95 and Counting: My Cup of Life

by

Robert J. McAllister M.D., Ph.D.

The contents of this work, including, but not limited to, the accuracy of events, people, and places depicted; opinions expressed; permission to use previously published materials included; and any advice given or actions advocated are solely the responsibility of the author, who assumes all liability for said work and indemnifies the publisher against any claims stemming from publication of the work.

All Rights Reserved
Copyright © 2016 by Robert J. McAllister M.D., Ph.D.

No part of this book may be reproduced or transmitted, downloaded, distributed, reverse engineered, or stored in or introduced into any information storage and retrieval system, in any form or by any means, including photocopying and recording, whether electronic or mechanical, now known or hereinafter invented without permission in writing from the publisher.

Dorrance Publishing Co
585 Alpha Drive
Suite 103
Pittsburgh, PA 15238
Visit our website at *www.dorrancebookstore.com*

ISBN: 978-1-4809-3017-9
eISBN: 978-1-4809-2995-1

TO THOSE WHO INSPIRED ME

Especially

JANE and LAURA

Preface

Last August I celebrated my 95th birthday, and today I decided to write another book. *Another book* sounds a little grandiose, but isn't that one of the perks of being an author? Don't want to make it sound like I wrote a full library. There were four books, serious subjects, not a lot of fun. Why a book now? Three reasons: 1.) I love to write. 2.) I'm getting tired of wasting time at the computer playing solitaire. 3.) I have buckets of thoughts I want to give "voice to." But I don't like to talk to people, even close family or friends, about many of my thoughts. Why not? I never was a "talker." In high school, my best friend's mother called me the "great stone face." I grew up on a ranch in Montana. Real cowboys aren't "talkers." My father was a quiet man and never cared for "blabbers." Reasons enough?

This book is going to cover chunks and pieces of my life, snippets if you will—, some serious, others not. People I knew. People who thought they knew me. Life experiences, mostly good, some painful, all now resolved or dissolved. Now is a peace-filled time in my life. I need to say so in words those I love can read and know it to be so.

Looking over the past from my current vantage point, I am filled with the knowledge everything I did in my life had its value in bringing me to where my life is today. And today is so filled with God's blessings I can honestly say there is nothing I wish for in my current life that I don't have. That statement might sound exaggerated and unusual for a 95 year old widower.

My daily prayer: "God, grant me continued health of body, mind and spirit and a pure heart until it is time to come home; then a peaceful death and reunion with Jane and all my loved ones in Your Kingdom." So I do have a wish, but in the form of a prayer.

Let me clarify one item now: Jane was the one true love of my life, God's excelling in generosity. We shared our life, our love, our faith, our joys and our tears for fifty years. She died of Alzheimer's three years and eleven days ago. No, I don't count the days; I see it noted on the calendar on my desk. I cannot wish to have her back, not to the sad, frightening, uncertain world in which she was living. So, the one thing I would wish for, I cannot. I often think Jane influences some of my decisions. She always did, and rightly so. Did Jane perhaps suggest another book at this time to keep my mind occupied with something other than her death? Could be. If you find such things impossible to believe, perhaps you will not agree with much of what I write.

I must tell you up front I will frequently comment about my faith and my prayers. I'm not selling religion or faith or spirituality (those are all separate items) to anyone, but if I write honestly about my life, all three of those have been and still are an integral part.

Currently, I live in a Continued Care Retirement Community (CCRC) called Vantage House. That name will be used throughout the book. Jane and I providentially moved here almost 12 years ago. It was a sudden, almost impulsive, decision. We did not know Jane had Alzheimer's, but it soon became evident as we faced the task of accommodating to a new environment. Now each time I see new residents moving in, boxes stacked high covering available floor space, my thought is: "You'll only need one box when you move out." Jane's ashes are in a cinerarium beside my desk. We never had double beds, but this box has double containers. I need someone to break through the dividing walls when I get my bunk.

What makes me think you want to know all this? I should tell you now I am going to write rather freely about many things that have happened in my life and many things I've done. I'm writing what I want to write with a sense of freedom that is moderately exhilarating! No expectations claim me. I have no particular goal. There are no deadlines. *Well, none I'm aware of.* If you see this as a selfish endeavor, perhaps it is. I've had what I believe are some unusual experiences in my life which make for reasonably good storytelling. You've heard the story of the two psychiatrists on the elevator at the end of the day. One says how exhausted he is from listening to patients all day.

The other replies with a shrug, "Who listens?"

As I sit here writing, perhaps I should ask, "Who reads?" However if one enjoys the writing, it is not because someone is reading. Writing has intrinsic rewards: igniting thoughts, ferreting words, teasing ideas. So even if you decide not to do the reading, I will enjoy the writing. And it keeps my mind working.

I must decide on some order for all the thoughts that bombard me since the idea of writing a book came to me. Pieces of my life still hang together sufficiently well to make a tapestry of certain episodes. The major tapestries will be early life, early education, military service, graduate studies, and various pieces of my professional life. And cross threads of a marriage, five children, a divorce, another marriage and another child. Does that sound dismissive, belittling to liken people to cross threads in a tapestry? It is more the other way around. My family, the relationships I had and have are in truth the substance of my life. *What I did* is only a backdrop. Instead of a tapestry you may prefer to see it all as a patchwork quilt with special people holding it all together.

At this time, it would seem artificial to discuss my life in sequence of time. True, that's how I lived it. But that's not how it lives in me. There is a great deal of seemingly random associations as my mind wanders through corners and crevices of the past. Faces and events totally unconnected in time show up in the same frame, often colored with the same feelings.

You might say: "These are but the mental ramblings of a mildly to moderately cognitively impaired old man."

That could be, but I'm going to have a hell of a lot of fun writing about it. There was a cowboy song of years ago, "Don't Fence Me In." That's where I began in my life and that's where I am now. Let me freely wander the prairies, the valleys, the mountains of my youth as they become the classrooms, offices, hospitals and this pinnacle of final days.

There will be no actual chapters. How can one divide a life into chapters anyway? Things in life don't just stop because we move away or say goodbye or death intervenes. What was, still is! Perhaps of less value, perhaps of greater value, but **there somewhere**. What we desire to forget may uncomfortably remain. The bell was rung. It will resonate forever in our inner ear. But the treasures of the past! Those people, those happenings, those moments that live in the tabernacle of our heart. Ah! Lasting blessings!

No actual chapters? Let's have "virtual chapters." Readers want to see books with prearranged "stopping places." A "Table of Contents" with chapter titles suggest the author knew where he was going and wanted to present a map of the entire terrain for the reader. Conclusion: since I don't really know where

I'm going I cannot provide some sort of GPS with meaningful chapter titles. But breaks, divisions, stopping places are still important and must be considered.

Let me establish an arbitrary pathway to chapter titles. Since I finished my last book, *An Alzheimer's Love Story*, in 2012, I've been writing articles for the in-house resident-produced paper called *Vantage Views*. I plan to include those articles in this book together with a few others things I've written. Some people tell me they're good, my friends tell me they're great. The editor calls me the in-house philosopher. Decide for yourself their value.

My plan is to begin each chapter with one of these articles which are each roughly two pages in length. The title of the article will provide the chapter title. When the article ends, I will just take off into the wild blue yonder of my ninety-five years and write freely and *with no particular relationship to the article you just finished reading*. I will separate the article from my continued writing with extra space and a series of pluses across the page. Example below.

+ + + + + + + + + +

Back to the text itself. Let's call these mental meanderings "lessons of life." We know that *being presented with lessons* doesn't always mean they are *learned lessons*. Especially true of life! No, wait, wait. Let's change that from "lessons of life" to "leaves from a tree of life." I'm not trying to teach anything. "Leaves" gives me more freedom. What I write about can probably be divided into categories (for those who like to have things sort of tidy in bags or boxes). I'll suggest the categories and the reader can decide which leaf goes into which bag. By the way, I am grateful those leaves are as fresh and green as they are. As time goes on, I expect they will gradually lose their vitality and one by one drop off my tree of consciousness. I hope my writing doesn't continue long enough for you to decide that's what's happening on my tree. Maybe you should have an extra bag for compost, just in case.

Every day I thank God for the gift of my faith and perseverance, so **Spirituality** is a category. My prayers probably touch on all the "categories of importance." I thank God for the family I'm from and the family I have, for teachers, mentors, classmates, and friends who have been and still are positive influences in my life. Add a category of **People**. Daily I ask blessings on those who were my students, those who attended my lectures and workshops, those who were my patients, and those who read or have read my books or articles. Eventually those prayers will include you, unless you stop reading and throw the book away. If you just put the unfinished book on the shelf, I'll keep you on the list. If you don't think prayers are of any value in this world, I will not try to convince you otherwise. Add a category of **Professional Life**. On the first page I mentioned my gratitude for health of body, mind and spirit. There will be some comments about diet, routine exercise, and physical activities past and present. So we'll add a category of **Health**.

My writing will be random, often the product of my solitary and somewhat contemplative afternoon walks. The subject matter may include events or thoughts about youthful cowboy days, graduate studies, military service, psychiatric practice, lecture halls, administrative duties, forensic involvements, or random incidents that come to mind. There are likely to be some opinions I have formed on a variety of topics. From my perspective, these categories cannot be seen as orderly containers with clear borders. The clear edges, the boundaries, the neat compartments I grew up thinking were the rigid boundaries of life became blurred by the intricacies and complexities of "living."

Let me add one additional item to keep you from going crazy or from thinking I'm already there. When I change subject matter, I will try not to do it in the middle of a paragraph. As I'm bouncing from one area of my life to another, you might find it irritating. I do not want to add to the frustrations of your life. To avoid all this, I will give you a signal of "topic change" by adding some extra space and an asterisk (*) when I'm moving to another subject.

Another advantage that accrues to me as writer: If I repeat a story you are less likely to remember my telling it before, because I am skipping around so much. If it ends up you don't know whether I'm confused or you're confused, blame me.

So much for the ground rules.

A poem I wrote for my 95th:

BIRTHDAY

Turning 95 is no great feat
Sit down, relax, have a seat.
I'll say again it's no reason to brag
Adding years only increases the sag.
Growing so old a person might rot
The alternate course I'd rather not.

Chapter One:
It's About Time

We all live under the umbrella: Is there time enough for this? For that? For plans? For dreams? The young voice impatience with the passage of time and want the next month, the next year, adulthood *now*. In old age, time becomes more significant but increasingly illusive. Simply put, the Weber-Fechner Law of physics states: "An increment is judged relative to the previous amount." This helps clarify our changing perception of time. When a child is ten, an incremental year is equal to one tenth of his or her lifetime and thus judged by the child to be a lo-o-o-ong time. When one is age ninety, another year is but one ninetieth of one's previous life, and thus glides by, and almost unexpectedly we are, yes, a year older.

We refer to segments of time measured in years. Time has another dimension and takes on a new reality when we use days to take the pulse of life. For the young, time measured in years wheels slowly. But days fly by precipitately with unfinished homework, unanswered text messages, and an untidy room because "I didn't have enough time!" In our older years, the months pass by with little recognition except a dutiful turn of the calendar page. But days can drag wearisomely.

There is a hint of incongruity in all of this *time* talk. The unvarnished truth is, at age ten and at age ninety, the day and the hour, every measured moment is the same. Clocks tick to the same rhythm all over the world but the music of life is not consistently legato.

A brief quiz: What characteristic of the young is no longer a centerpiece of our lives? What makes their days disappear before they're finished with them? The answer, *activity!* They are not just active, they are hyperactive. As a result, many of them are wrongly diagnosed with Hyperactive Disorder. They are, by nature, overly active and their involvement in a million (well, at least ten) things at the same time scatters their thoughts like a flock of birds searching for a lost worm (or in this case lost homework).

Most of us have lived *busy* lives in the past. The "previous amount" of activity filled our day, sometimes overflowing into evening hours. So, what happens when we spend (or waste perhaps) our day time hours in idleness? Our previous level of activity not only filled our time but fulfilled the deeply planted human need to do, to plan, to contribute, to expand, and to grow. Inactivity relative to the previous amount of activity leaves us with an unwelcome and unsettling disquietude, void, and imbalance. An increase of activity diminishes the mound of inner discomfort related to the loss of our previously active life.

In the busyness of your prior lifetime how many times can you recall thinking, "If only I had more time?" In that other world, "free time" was a luxury, often jealously guarded from undue invasion by an employer, a neighbor, a friend, a child, and at times even a spouse. Ah! The quietude! The peace! The freedom in that little space of existence that was your very own! It was characteristic of those years to "save time," as if we believed it could be stored and its later availability would allow fulfillment of those dreams of traveling, reading, playing, and enjoying life in a variety of ways.

And now we find ourselves "time-wealthy," wondering how to spend our late life treasures, which unexpectedly present now as less alluring, less gracious. After waiting patiently during those years of busyness, age intrudes boldly and often brazenly into our world and begins stealthily but steadily, not only to reduce our stores of time, but with unseemliness to limit our ability to spend what remains in our account.

Now the contradiction: the more time we spend actively, the more time we are likely to have. If we use our time doing nothing, we not only lose the time, but lose the significance inherent in its very reality. Perhaps a careful look at the Vantage House Weekly Bulletin will stir some thoughts, awaken some dreams, and incite some interests. Resultant activity could well bring brighter, *shorter* days replete with a new sense of the value of life and the worth *you* contribute to it.

95 and Counting: My Cup of Life

+ + + + + + + + + +

Perhaps I should give some brief, and I trust reasonably accurate, details of the structure that framed my being in this world. My father and mother were pioneers in Montana with mother arriving the year before Montana achieved statehood (1889). Paternal grandparents were from Ireland, maternal grandparents from Norway. Dad and Mom's homestead grew into a 2,800 acre wheat farm/cattle ranch. I grew up in a five a.m. to nine p.m. work world, youngest of seven boys and one girl. There were horses, no tractors to pull the binders, the mowers, the hay wagons, the plows, the drills, the rakes, and the grain wagons. Nothing was motorized except the car and an old steam engine used to run the twenty-four-inch table saw for cutting trees into fence posts and firewood. I joined the field crews at age ten, driving a team on a hay rake.

•

A clear, never to be forgotten memory: I was raking freshly mowed hay in the meadow near a wide stream, willows scattered on the banks and morning glories freshly blooming in the cool of early day. The sun was soft and the breeze gently teasing. I stopped the horses and sat there several minutes captured by the overwhelming beauty and *feel* of the scene. I was absorbed, enclosed in a sacred place; nature reached out and embraced me. My childhood mind told me *God is here*.

Now, when I walk around the lake near Vantage House, there is a precise spot on the north end where I stop on the wooden bridge. Framed by two trees, all I see is the lake, the sky, harboring trees, maybe a heron, a duck, a wren, no buildings, no cars, and no people. And I'm back near the flowing creek and the morning glories. And I never feel closer to God than during those few minutes. All the years, all the miles, all the relationships are tied in the bundle of one small life. And it is mine. These two events, separated by eight-three years, are the blink of an eye apart. Yes, perhaps a lifetime is but a moment.

Of course I believe God is always with me and I strive for an increasing awareness of God's presence. But there are those moments when I am aware of being surrounded by God's Being, the presence of "Who am."

•

You see how I digress. I return to put together some few pieces of my life as background. At age eight, I went to a Catholic boarding school fifty miles from home. The closing of the nearby one room school house because of too few students, and the closing of county roads because of too much winter snow, forced the decision. Homesickness is not like any other loss and often brought nighttime tears. I used to dream there was a short-cut to the ranch, but no one would ever try my route. Boarding school closed when I was twelve or thirteen and I lived in a variety of situations for a few years based on availability and cost. Those were hard times.

For a couple of years, I lived with the school janitor and cleaned classrooms after school to help pay the keep. During the last two years of high school, I lived completely unsupervised in a rough and tumble workingman's boarding house. That experience contributed its share to my verbal reticence. I felt "out of place" as I often do in social situations. To earn spending money I set bowling pins in a nearby bowling alley from six p.m. until midnight Fridays and Saturdays. The pins were set by hand in those days.

After finishing high school, I was off to Loras College in Dubuque, Iowa to study for the priesthood; arrangements and tuition were provided by the Catholic Diocese of Great Falls. First time I was ever more than fifty miles from the ranch. I was the only student from the west, a real hick from the sticks. Again, I felt out of place. Someone named me "Ace" because of the cowboy background. I still find old books with "Ace" inside the cover.

After graduation from Loras, I went to St. Edward's Seminary in Seattle for two years. I decided not to stay, so I left and joined the service. Basic training was in Mississippi, then to Patton's army in Europe, finally arriving in Linz, Austria near Camp Mathausen, which was liberated by the 11th Armored Division. Camp Mathausen, nicknamed "The Bone Grinder", was the largest labor camp of the war and was used mostly for extermination of the intelligentsia through labor in quarries, mines and munition factories. While doing guard duty near the camp, I saw flatbed trucks hauling naked emaciated bodies to burial sites. Simon Wiesenthal, the post-war Nazi hunter, was a survivor of that camp and other camps.

During basic training and in combat, there was always a spirit of comradery, a sense of service to God and country, and always the goal of victory. But the army of occupation was, for me, an unsavory, dissolute, and disheartening life—POW camps, Displaced Person (DP) camps, Mathausen, destruction and decay, disorder and death everywhere. It was a nightmare. I lost my bearings, my compassion, and my dreams. (If you regard a lampshade made of human skin a curiosity and not an abomination, then you have lost your compassion). To reverse the slide into my personal hell and get back on track I volunteered for the Pacific and was sent to Marseille, France for embarkation. But while I waited in Marseille the war ended in the Pacific. Once more an unsavory, dissolute and disheartening life.

    I married a Swiss girl, was discharged in Paris, and returned with my new wife to the Montana ranch. After one year, I was off to the Catholic University of America in Washington, D.C., earning a Ph. D. in Psychology. Then I went to Georgetown for a medical degree followed by a year of internship and three years of psychiatric residency. I had five children by the time I began practice at age 41. My early professional work included teaching in the School of Social Work, consulting at the Marriage Counseling Service, and at the Child Guidance Clinic—all at Catholic University.

    In 1966 I divorced, became Superintendent of the Nevada State Hospital in Reno, and married Jane that fall. We moved to Grant Pass, Oregon in 1971, and then to Spokane, Washington in 1976 where I taught at Gonzaga University. In 1985 we came to Baltimore where I worked at Taylor Manor Psychiatric Hospital and taught at Loyola University. In 1992, we moved to Maine and after one year returned to Ellicott City, Md. Over the course of the years, I had private practices in Takoma Park, Md., Grants Pass, Ore., Spokane, Wash. and Ellicott City, Md. In 2003, Jane and I moved into Vantage House in Columbia, Md. I discontinued private practice in December 2005 and teaching in 2007.

•

A bit about ranch life. It was primitive and poor; it was hard work and long hours; it was challenging and wonderful. At an early age, I felt I was an integral part of it all. By age eight, I was part of the yard crew composed of my father, five brothers and at times hired men. I was the go-fer initially, but also began working in our two acre garden, which meant endless hoeing, picking potato bugs, hilling corn, and picking weeds. By age ten, I was on my horse six days a week, morning and evening, taking the work horses to and from their pasture and working in the fields during the day. Work not only strengthened me physically but instilled a reality-based sense of my value to others and to the world. At an early age, *I was being productive*; *I was contributing*. That sense, that need has been with me all my life and its nagging brings me to this writing. Do I regret those years? Would I change them in any way? They remain the platform of all that makes life worthwhile.

I can't, well I can, but I won't, keep myself from commenting on one of the missing pieces in the lives of most youngsters these days. Young people need to have a solid and deeply rooted awareness of their worth as human beings, not just as a son or daughter or as a student. Parents and teachers are an important part of instilling a sense of self-worth, but planting the seed is not enough. The seed must be nurtured and mature and it does when the individual becomes part of a positive group, a worthy cause to which they know they contribute. Involvement with negative, hostile or toxic companions retards growth and destroys the potential.

•

Diet has become a focus of health concerns these days. Our diet on the ranch probably violated many current recommendations. It included whole (fresh from the cow) milk, almost daily fresh whole eggs, lots of cream, lots of butter, lots of beef, pork, and chickens all home grown. We had garden vegetables, fresh in summer, and then canned by mother for winter eating. Fresh fruit was rare except in the fall when the harvest came in from Oregon orchards. The only fish was cod in those neat wooden boxes. We ate prairie chickens, pheasants, and deer meat in season and occasionally out of season when one came within handy range. After the war, during the year I spent on the ranch I shot pigeons. There's not much meat unless you shoot them in the head. I could do that.

My diet is markedly different now—less red meat, no cream, no butter, skim milk, more Mediterranean I would say. I have mild hypertension well controlled with one medicine. My cardiovascular system apparently suffered no harm from my earlier diet. I don't know if my present diet has salutary effects or not.

I thank God every day for my physical health. Do I think God gives me that health? Not directly. God gives me the ability and the spirit to exercise regularly and eat properly, and apparently the lineage of good genes. Yes, I know, God is the potter and I am the clay. But clay has accidents as well as substance. Some is not as malleable as others. Check with Thomas Aquinas about substance and accidents. I like to think of God as the Master Builder who provides us with a tool kit of our own. We need to learn to use the tools in the endowment of our humanity.

•

Have to write this now! Just got back from a wonderful walk around the lake. Temperature +17, wind-chill -2, wind 20-30 mph. Glorious walk. Beautiful sun, blue sky, fresh snow. It connected me with grade and high school days, walking to school in winter. Everyone walked to school. Catholic schools had no buses. Schools never closed for snow that I remember. Snow came in November and stayed until March. So today was one of those experiences that bundles pieces of life 80 years apart into the same tapestry. The experience today was exciting, freeing from the drab interior of the closeted world and carrying me on the eagle wings of a strong wind whipping through the tall bare trees. When I ran with the wind at my back, it felt like I could fly.

The lake today was spectacular and a pictogram of life. Part water, part ice with delicate swirls of snow in soft flowing patterns of curves and circles and solid portions. "God's winter Rorschach." It tells it all! The icy realities of everyday living support the ever changing configuration of life events that hold us captive for a space of time—beautiful, harsh, delicate, and temporary. And in between the ice floes, the cold water of the impatient River Styx waiting to receive it all and carry it off to another world.

•

The walk recalled and wrapped me in those precious years of education and the warmth and comfort not just of learning, but of finding my strengths in the classroom. The same spirit that prompted my walk today propelled me in my pursuit of education. That spirit was passed to me from two hard working loving parents. It sprouted in our garden and matured in the hay fields and the wheat fields of Montana. In my daily prayers, I thank God for my parents and "the values and virtues they taught me."

•

The walk also brought back boyhood memories of Montana and precious hours spent on the ranch during winter vacations. The great satisfaction in wintertime was the hunkering down that occurred. Playing cards with my father and brothers, listening to Amos and Andy on the battery powered radio, regularly digging a path to the outhouse through the mountains of snow. Fording our way to the barns to feed the pigs, cows and chickens, and to milk twice a day. Oats and hay for the saddle horses kept in the corral. A load of hay taken to the cattle in the fields. As I walked today, my mind was filled not just with the bare memories, but with the feel of it all: the chill of the air, the bite of the wind, the whiteness that only belongs to snow. What a blessed and rich experience as a child and now again! The harmony and simplicity of it all, the peace of life's connectedness!

Last fall as winter crept closer with shorter days and cooling temperatures, I wondered how I could possibly manage another season of cold and snow. To my surprise, it becomes increasingly welcome. In some way, I have become more connected with the childhood challenges winter used to bring. It is one more thing that connects me with my early life and once more packages 95 years into a neat continuum.

•

Most people pray, even if it's only in emergencies. But I think very few people talk to God. There are only two people I ever knew who I believe talked to God. One was my father. In the little town (Geyser), six miles from the ranch, we went to Sunday Mass. It was a small church with seating capacity of about a hundred. I vividly remember, I can see him now, my father kneeling in prayer before Mass. I was probably four or five. He looked at the altar so totally focused, lips moving, oblivious to all around him. My thought was as clear as the words I write. "He's talking to God."

The other person who I believe "talked to God" was Jane. She had no meaningful religious education. She lived with her mother and maternal grandparents. She was the only "practicing Catholic" in the house. Her grandmother took her to Mass every Sunday and returned to get her after. The two of them said Jane's prayers together every night. In spite of that sparse background, she appeared to fit God comfortably into her life and, I would surmise, God took her comfortably into God's life.

I consider myself a good Catholic and the feeling goes back through all my years with some significant doubts creeping in during a few slippery episodes, now resolved and absolved. I was always a little envious of what I saw as Jane's "first name basis" relationship with God. I always felt her religion was "written on her heart." Would that were true of mine. Before and during her illness, Jane would occasionally tell me something God said to her. She was not hallucinating. She was not delusional. I wouldn't say she heard God's voice, but she clearly got God's messages. I think she may have argued with God on occasion, and I'm at loss to know how it turned out.

Early in her illness, Jane wrote *Before It's Too Late*, her life story (with considerable assistance and encouragement from me). During her illness, she continued writing little personal bits on any available piece of paper. One of her written notes: "I talk to God constantly as I have always done. I have stopped asking 'why'." The "why" was about Alzheimer's. Another note: "God hold my face in your hands." Beautiful, intimate prayerfulness!

•

A question comes: Does what I am experiencing regularly happen to people as they approach the end of life? Is this *the circle of life?* It all feels so satisfying, so fulfilling as I now consider it. It borders on mysterious, sublime. Even as I ask the question, comes the obvious answer. Among my fellow residents here I see many walkers, wheelchairs, and canes. There are those who see poorly or not at all; those for whom hearing aids are not sufficient. And then the many who have difficulty organizing their thoughts, finding where they want to go, or recognizing those they see. Life's circle has only one uniform ending. We start with helplessness and end where we began. Where I am now brings me humility and wonder.

Chapter Two: Quality of Life

This phrase is spoken easily and casually, but often without much depth of meaning. It almost sounds like a "catchphrase," it comes so glibly in conversations and in the world of advertising. This new car, this new skin product, this new vitamin, this new iPad will improve your "quality of life." Unfortunately, those three words have a deep attraction for people, perhaps because we all have lives the quality of which could be improved. In fact, is not the worthy goal of life to improve its quality?

People rarely boast about their quality of life. They may say they have a good life, a satisfying life, but *quality* suggests "a degree of excellence" which stretches into a world they still strive for, no matter how much success surrounds them. At least in fantasy there is always a higher rung.

What is the reality behind this phrase so easily bandied about? What gives life quality? Our quick and superficial answers might strike the same note, but perhaps not in the same key: good health, a happy family, good friends, and financial security. And what else? A spiritual component? Secret desires? Daydreams of grand ventures? And what about the fine points of these items? Would we agree a good diet, exercise, an adequate and regular sleep pattern add quality to our life? Or not so important? Would we agree that tenderness, compromise, faithfulness, and sacrifice add quality to life? Or is that excessive? Good friends, what kind, how many? Some of us are gregarious, others more solitary. Is financial security having enough to see us through our lifetime? Or are children an integral part of that picture?

Indeed it seems obvious each person would describe a *quality of life* special to their own needs, their own life history, and their own distinct personality. There is a conclusion. The composite of ingredients to achieve the desired quality is unique for each person. It follows then that each person should conscientiously realize how inappropriate and perhaps damaging it can be to impose one's own *quality of life concept* on another person. What's good for the goose is not always good for the gander.

It is probably accurate to say every resident at Vantage House is here because of a diminishment in quality of life. The move is usually made in order to minimize the deleterious effect of some change, assumed to be irreversible. The change may be subtle, perhaps only a growing concern about the future as one confronts the reality of aging. The change may be serious health challenges destined to be increasingly debilitating. In making such a move, we relinquish at least a bit of the quality associated with independence.

But there are serious and significant losses in our community, loss of mobility being the most apparent and most severe. Failing eyesight, hearing loss, arthritis, diabetes and other health losses common to our age group take their toll on quality. It is remarkable to observe how graciously and courageously individuals cope in such circumstances. While one stands in awe, one can only assume they call on other assets of mental and emotional strength and perhaps deep faith.

The thought arises: what can I do to help others who experience such losses? A friendly attitude, a ready smile, a pleasant greeting, the *offer* of a friendly hand. On occasion even these may seem unwelcome. We may try to help someone rise from a chair, unaware the person's quality of life may be enhanced by getting up on their own. Think about it! Sometimes help is unwelcome. *We cannot assume we know what might enhance the quality of life for another.*

Emotional needs are an intrinsic ingredient of life's quality. Our heart hungers, not the heart that bleeds but the heart that needs, that needs the warmth, the words, the smile, the touch, the face, the memory that breathes meaning into our existence this day and the next and the next.

A small loss for most of us is mildly impaired memory. For others, severe memory loss has come like a thief in the night and stolen much of their treasured past, clouded their present, and left them with an empty future. Their river of life no longer flows. Their memory is like stagnant unconnected pools of muddied water. A familiar activity, the gentle word of an aide, a smiling unrecognized face, and a kind touch are like fresh water, but soon to be lost in the dark pool of forgetfulness. Quality of life so briefly improved! Good physical care, an emotionally calming and comforting environment are essential, but no special program will make the river flow again.

+ + + + + + + + + +

Almost every day the news carries an article about a murder and the question of mental illness is raised by some reporter. Subjects reported on the news often stir memories of events long gone from our lives. Here's a case for you to judge; have a go at it. It's a case about a woman with whom I spent approximately one hour in a jail cell about forty-five years ago and for whom I now pray daily. Maybe it's not inappropriate to place this story after the "Quality of Life" heading.

•

A brief sidebar: Before I explain about the prayers and about the woman, let me broach another matter. When I write about people, I do not do so to exhibit my own behavior other than is necessary to give meaning and substance to the tale. I ask you, the reader, to reflect on your reactions to, your feelings about the people to whom I introduce you. What response stirs inside you as their stories intrude into your thoughts: compassion, anger, doubt, pity, fear, dislike, disdain, affection, what? Try to remember how the story resonated within you. Yes, there will be a quiz in a later chapter. Of those presented, which were the most appealing to you? Multiple choice with several right answers and several others you may want to cancel if you choose them.

I speak about prayer often as I write. I do not boast I am pious or holy because I pray. That reminds me of St. Paul who seems a bit on the boastful side but then protests a couple of times, "I am not boasting." Prayer has become increasingly important in my life as I search for meaning and continuing stability now my life companion is gone. My prayer life increased during Jane's illness as I pleaded with God to allow me to care for her until her death. God generously answered that prayer. Now my first prayer of the day lasts approximately an hour, not on my knees or in some prayer posture, but as I exercise robot-like.

This morning prayer reviews not only the segments of my life but it is a time of remembering events and naming significant people in each period. It is a time when I thank God for the multitude of blessings God has given me. I sometimes wonder if this is an attempt to wrap my life into one spiritual whole, a package of all the years neatly tied with prayer to present to my Maker—as if life could be so neat and tidy. In the prayers I include many people by name, people from the past and the present.

•

For this woman (of forty-five years ago) I have no name other than "the woman from the jail."

When I was Superintendent of the Nevada State Hospital for the Mentally Ill, I became close friends with a Reno judge, Tom Craven. Tom called one day to say he had just seen a woman in his court who was charged with murdering her neighbor. She refused to utter a word to him or to anyone else. Would I see her?

She was seated when I entered her cell. I sat on the bench near her. I quietly explained why I was there and asked if she would talk to me a little about what recently happened in her life. I sat with her for fifteen or twenty minutes, gently encouraging her to talk, but allowing periods of lengthy silence. My voice was soft, reassuring, and calm. She was mute and did not look at me except when I entered the cell. Finally, I said I needed to be going and might not be able to return. I called for the guard. As he unlocked the cell door, the woman made a noise, not a word just a throated noise. I went back and sat by her and helped her release her story.

When she was a teenager living with her parents, her father was the mayor of a western city. When he ran for a second term, there was a "communist group" who bitterly and vehemently opposed him. He lost the election. Within a few years, she went off to college and later married. She and her husband moved to Reno and for several years had been best friends with the couple who lived across the street, Charlie and his wife. Charlie worked in the maintenance crew at the hospital. I knew him well.

Years ago, the woman had decided the "communists" were responsible for her father's defeat, and she began to think about and worry about their power. As time went on, she began to believe communists were following her, spying on her. The misgivings grew into fears, and eventually paranoid delusions with a threatening quality. (Reader: remember these were the days of the McCarthy Hearings before Congress and also the days of Rev. Fulton Sheen's diatribes on The Catholic Hour, radio and later TV, about communists. The news and how it is presented clearly influences thinking and beliefs especially of the vulnerable).

The woman, her husband, Charlie, and his wife spent a Saturday evening at Harrah's Club in Reno, an outing they frequently shared. During the evening, the woman became suspicious that Charlie's wife was slyly communicating with "certain strangers" in the club. The woman spent a restless night harboring increasing fears. Sunday morning she saw Charlie's wife come out on her porch across the street and pick up the morning paper. By then, the woman *knew* Charlie's wife was in league with the communists, and by picking up the paper had signaled them to come and kill her. She got a butcher knife, walked across the street, and when Charlie's wife responded to her knock, she stabbed her to death.

After the court received my report, she was sent to the State Hospital until able to stand trial. I did not see her again because of administrative duties, nor would it have been appropriate. When I left Reno she was still in the hospital but improved and her psychiatrist was ready to recommend she go to trial. I never knew the result of the trial.

So what do you think? Guilty or not? Quickly, because I must move on. Had I testified based on the one interview, I would certainly have said she knew the difference between right and wrong and knew her action was, in itself, wrong, but she believed she was defending her own life against a murderous enemy. Not guilty by reason of severely diminished capacity; diagnosis: paranoid schizophrenia.

Why do I pray for her? I'm not sure. It was a moving experience; I would say a sacred experience to be privy to the secrets that hauntingly grew in her mind for years, and the bold and terrible act born of her paranoia. Perhaps I pray for her because she gave me the gift of her confidence, she allowed me to unlock the cellar of her fears; she permitted me to lead her across the boundary separating her from the real world. I was her guide; I held her hand. She rewarded my patience and responded to my compassion. I pray because I want her to be at peace after all those years of torment.

•

A couple of years earlier, we had a seventeen year old boy (an only child) admitted to the hospital. Glen came from Lovelock, a small town near Reno. (Locals used to say it's better to be out of wedlock than out of Lovelock). On a nice summer day after his father left for work, Glen got his rifle and went to hunt squirrels but without success. When he came back in the house, he shot and killed his mother. Just like that. Probably because he was a minor, he was admitted to the hospital for evaluation and treatment. He was there about one year. After people got to know him, he was allowed on the grounds and used to work with our grounds' crew. I wasn't aware of all that was negotiated with the courts, but he was discharged from the hospital and allowed to join either AmeriCorps or a similar program.

There was no history of violence or abuse in the family and no history of unusual behavior in Glen, who continually maintained he *did not know* why he shot his mother. I don't think he did know. I truly doubt he will ever know. We've all done things, and as we think about it later, we can't really explain why we did it.

You might say, "Not so."

When driving, did you ever change lanes for no particular reason and if asked why, you would say:

"I don't know. What difference does it make?"

In conversation, have you ever made a remark totally out of place and embarrassing to everyone, and then realized you had no idea why you said it? Everyone, perhaps teenagers especially, act without thinking. I know changing traffic lanes or making an inappropriate comment is far from killing someone. But it is important to realize and acknowledge the fact that sometimes our minds do function independently of our intentions and thoughts.

Here I report our consulting psychologist at the hospital did an evaluation. In his desire to be poetic or pedantic (I know not which), he closed his report with the following: "Glen calls to mind the famous case: 'Lizzie Borden took an axe and gave her mother forty whacks. When she saw what she had done, she gave her father forty-one'." There was absolutely no foundation for his bizarre conclusion other than to flash his own ego. More about this man in a later segment.

This is also an example of the vagaries of life. At the Governor's Christmas party and with the case pending, I heard someone ask a judge his opinion about the case.

The judge's response: "Killed his mother and just as likely to kill his father."

All based on the psychologist's whimsy. How irresponsible! How unprofessional! The power wielded by words!

During my time in Reno, I served on the Parole Board of the Nevada State Prison. The warden's typical question of those seeking parole:

"Why did you commit the crime?" Whatever the prisoner's answer, the warden's invariable and somewhat sadistic response was, "That's an excuse not a reason."

Glen didn't even have an excuse. It was rare anyone got paroled. At that time in Nevada, men who had committed a crime and required hospitalization were hospitalized in the prison. The state required they see a psychiatrist once a month. Since I went to the prison anyway, I assumed that duty. The place was a study in sadism.

Reno, I suppose, had an average small city level of crime. A gambling story came to the hospital. A Californian, addicted to gambling and broke, stole some of his parents belongings and sold them to "regain his gambling losses" at a Lake Tahoe Club. After losing his stash at the tables, he drew a pistol and threatened to kill himself. The club could not tolerate the possible publicity. He was arrested on the charge of holding the club hostage and was sent to the state hospital, not for evaluation, but for treatment. Evaluation might have required information to the court, again endangering news leaks. There was no evidence of serious illness. We kept him a couple of weeks, and then transported him back to California with the recommendation he attend Gamblers Anonymous. The story never hit the press!

Besides the murder of the employee's wife, the hospital had its own tragedies. About four months before I left my position as Superintendent, I hired a new psychiatrist who brought his young teenage son with him. Staff psychiatrists were provided a house on grounds. The "son" was rarely seen. Many wondered about the situation. A few months after I left, the psychiatrist killed himself and the youngster. I never heard anything further about the case.

Before I leave the hospital, I will mention a second sad event, this one on a ward. A physically and mentally challenged ("retarded" was the term in those days) boy of about ten fatally strangled in a restraining harness. Jane and I were away from the hospital for the day. We were sightseeing with my visiting brother and his wife. The parents of the boy came to the hospital with a gun determined to shoot the Superintendent. The State Police were looking for me all day. They didn't find me but neither did the parents. It was of course headline news. Records indicated the parents had not visited the boy for years, but suddenly he was the greatest treasure in their lives. There was never a lawsuit as far as I knew. I suspect it was settled out of court.

For clarification, I should mention the hospital not only housed the mentally ill of the state, but also the mentally challenged requiring institutional care. The two groups were housed in separate buildings.

•

You'll be tired of my lake walks. But this one was unusual. Probably the most thrilling walk I've had since Jane died. If she were here, we'd have been out there together. On Saturdays, I usually go to the Shrine of St. Anthony for noon Mass. Snow was predicted for today and started about 10:30 a.m. I didn't want to drive in the snow. I decided to walk to the lake. Temp around twelve above, moderate wind, and snowing. It was somewhat challenging. No other walkers, no other tracks in the snow. And on return, the tracks I had made in going were filled with new snow. At times, the snow was almost blinding. Buildings across the lake, a distance of 100 to 150 yards, were hardly visible. When I stopped at my "shrine spot" I deliberated about continuing. On the one hand, I have confidence God watches over me. On the other hand, I believe God wants me to use the tools in my tool box. There was really no danger so I continued my solitary outing around the lake.

•

The snow blowing in my face reminded me of a boyhood dictum. If you're out on the prairie on horseback and a blizzard catches you and you can't see where you're going, give the horse his rein and he'll take you home. Horseback in wintertime is always dangerous. A horse can slip on ice or suddenly come into snow too deep to navigate at a fast pace. If the horse falls, the rider's foot in the stirrup can be caught underneath. A foot or ankle fracture can easily result. Then you're fortunate if you have a horse with sense enough not to run and leave you there.

The other danger in winter: the temperature might be forty degrees when you leave the barn. A fairly light jacket is adequate. By the time you reach the cattle, the weather may have changed to ten below zero. Weather changes rapidly in Montana winters. Fast-moving blinding blizzards are not uncommon.

Why would I tell you about horses and Montana winters? That's probably of little interest to you. But it was an important part of my life and I savor the memories.

•

A little about my mother. She was a quiet, charitable, loving, gentle, somewhat shy, small, almost frail appearing woman, but a powerful worker. I don't think I ever heard her utter an uncharitable remark about anyone, and when someone else did, she defended. In our little church, there was, hanging above and back of the altar, a large round frame with a picture of the Sorrowful Mother. It's a picture of Jesus' Mother Mary, with a blue veiled head turned to the left in a lowered, sad posture. Probably about the same age when I watched my father pray, I asked my mother why the woman in the picture looked so sad. Mom replied, "She's sad when little boys don't behave." Sometimes I pray I will not do anything that will make the Blessed Mother sad. You think it sounds childlike? I would say you're right. So, maybe I am a child of God.

•

Sex education was rather sparse in the world of my childhood. Sex education in the Catholic school translated into the word "purity." Most of us probably had some idea what "purity" was referring to, but we never talked about it. I don't think we knew how to talk about it. A few of the boys made sly reference to body parts, so we learned various words, but weren't always sure where they belonged. I can't say we were innocent. Sometimes it's hard to know the difference between innocent and ignorant. The closest I got to pornography was the Sears Roebuck Catalogue in the outhouse. We had some "hell fire and damnation" retreats given by the Redemptorist priests. I believe it was their specialty. They could make you lose sleep for just thinking about a girl.

My tender, reticent mother apparently decided I should have some sex education. I was probably ten plus.

One day when no one was around, she quietly said something like, "You should probably know something about sexual things, but you're around the cattle and you see what they do, so I don't need to talk about it." That sweet, dear woman must have used all the courage she could muster to say even that much.

We usually had two or three bulls to service (a livestock term) the herd of cows we kept. The bulls were kept separate from the cows except for the month of May and June. This was breeding season with the expectation calves would be born in late winter. Bulls could be vicious with each other and with anyone who might get in the way of their performing their duty. When not on duty, they could be even more cantankerous and fight with one another when there wasn't a cow to fight over. I became well aware of the coupling procedure of cattle. We kept no stallions but hired a stud horse when we wanted a mare bred. I was probably an early teen when I saw horses mating for the first time. Suffice it to say, it was a wild scene.

One of our bulls in some manner broke that small retractable appendage whereby he earned his keep. It was a bit unsightly. I always wondered how it happened, but no one was offering any explanation. After an on-site consultation with the local veterinarian, the bull was shipped to market. After my mother's sex talk, had I taken seriously the bull's injury, I might have considered staying in the seminary.

Chapter Three:
Oops!

When you hear that word, you assume someone made a mistake. Then your mind often goes to the tight knit little group of cells somewhere in your head that screams out loudly (inside your head of course) "disappear lest anyone know you too *make mistakes.*" We automatically think people will judge and remember our mistakes. How strangely our mind works at times! One word *"Oops"* sets our minds on edge, the edge of a precipice at the bottom of which lies all the mistakes we have tried to hide from ourselves for so long. It may be why some people want to point out other peoples' mistakes, to hide their own.

Let's take a careful look at this shadowed past which stares back at us. Indeed, mistakes are no reason for sleepless nights, chewed fingernails, an extra drink or piece of chocolate to quell a sense of desperation. The Oxford Dictionary says a mistake is "an action or judgment that is misguided or wrong; something that is not correct."

Probably we all own up to judgments that were off the mark, and we may do so with some embarrassment. (If anyone claims never to have misjudged a situation or another person, we will need to consult your friends and perhaps family members). Think of one or two of those errors of judgment. How do you know they were errors? You answer, "Look how it turned out. I should have known better." The point is you didn't know how it would turn out until after you did it. And you really don't know now how the alternatives would have turned out because they never happened, not for you anyway. The only way to avoid any errors of judgment is never to make any judgments and seriously limit your life!

Have mistakes ruined your life, destroyed your peace of mind? Perhaps for a period of time. But look a little closer. Are you sure things would be better for you today if you had made a different choice? How can you be so sure? Because you really don't know and never will know how a different choice would have affected your life. You can guess, imagine, and speculate, but you cannot know. You would have *to have lived* the other choice to know. There is no way to know the "mistake" of six or sixty years ago really did detract from your present life.

We've spoken about mistakes of "misguided" decisions. Don't think the word "misguided" gets you off the hook. You can try to blame someone else: parent, spouse, teacher, preacher, perhaps a smooth salesman. It won't fly. We're going to assume each person was responsible for his or her own behavior at least during your remembered past. There may be some extenuating circumstances now, but that's another subject.

The dictionary said: "misguided or wrong." *Wrong decisions* should be looked at under a different lens. Wrong decisions are wrong not because of the outcome but because of the decision process. *Something* other than judgment and reason is involved. That *something* clouds our judgment, beguiles our reasoning. "Not me," perhaps you say. Yes, you, unless you are a person without emotions. These wrong decisions (wrong because emotionally based) may turn out badly or may turn out well. We have all made decisions based on anger, fear, anxiety, love, pity, hatred, sadness. Strong emotions often bring quick decisions; some we live to regret. Others may be among the best decisions we ever made. The process was wrong not necessarily the decision.

Perhaps the ideal way to make decisions is calmly and carefully based on your best judgment, then stand back and assess your feelings. If it feels good, do it!

+ + + + + + + + + + +

I could go through my life and pick out examples of the "oops" theme *ad infinitum*. You probably can think of a few in your own life. But let me pick up on one of my major ones. This was a wrong decision made for all the wrong reasons and with contributing emotional components as wrong as they could be.

Did it turn out well? I said in the preface, "Everything I did in my life had its value in bringing me to where I am in my life today." So yes, it turned out well.

I told you how I felt about the army of occupation and then waiting in France for embarkation to the Pacific when the war ended. The army tried to ease our stay with some good programs. One involved a three or four day tour of Switzerland. Some of the details are no longer in my head, or more likely just can't be found up there. During the trip, I stopped in a jewelry store in Sion. A young attractive girl was behind the counter. I knew a few words in French; she none in English. I hung around showing my interest in knowing her better. Eventually, her brother came in to close the store for the day. He and I both knew a little German. He had been in the seminary so we could toss in a little Latin.

They invited me to dinner at their mother's house where they both lived. After dinner, I left and joined my tour companions. And I was in love and wanted to marry Marguerite and was determined to do so. Yes, that's what I said, and must admit that's truly what I thought. Back in Marseille, I wrote to her. She had a translator and wrote back and I had a translator, etc. I put my name in for another tour of Switzerland and probably had one scheduled within six or eight months. We walked around a bit with her brother Louis, and had dinner with her mother. I got a room in Sion for the night. Spent time with the three of them the next day and proposed with Louis as interpreter.

On my next trip to Switzerland two or three months later, Marguerite and I were married in the Catholic Church of Sion. Why would you be reading a book written by a crazy person? I know that's what you're thinking. I don't blame you. So, maybe you'll decide to read further expecting an explanation. I don't really have one. I think I avoided the question most of my life. In recent years, I've tried to come up with some kind of answer before cognitive senility really sets in. Here's the best I can do.

Remember how I felt about POW camps, DP camps, devastation, destruction, and the Holocaust. I had been out of touch with my whole world of family, friends, and faith. I had forgotten everything I knew of tenderness, compassion, or even conviction. The world was upside down and stagnant. It wasn't empty. No, it was full—of evil and wrong and bitterness and cruelty. It held a loneliness that could not be assuaged. And there was Switzerland, so clean, so beautiful, so pure, so well-ordered. A land of enchantment! I fell in love with a fantasy embodied in a Swiss girl behind a counter in a jewelry shop. That was the basis for my relationship with Marguerite.

I would guess, on her part, there may have been a different fantasy, perhaps that of many people in the world, "America, going to America, land of opportunity, of dreams!" I said above I was out of touch with faith. That's not quite correct. I still had my faith and practiced my religion. I had lost touch with my spirituality.

I talked to no one about my decision. There was really no one to talk to. When I spoke with my Lieutenant in Marseille to arrange for my discharge (which occurred in Paris) he asked:

"Are you sure you know what you're doing?"

Of course, I knew and thought he should mind his own business! I have in recent years wondered why Marguerite, her mother and her brother could so readily agree to her going off with a G.I. with whom she had spent only twelve or fifteen hours in a minimal exchange of piecemeal conversation.

On return to the U.S., Marguerite and I lived on the ranch one year before we went to the District of Columbia for my studies at Catholic U. and later Georgetown. I became quite adept at French and Marguerite followed later with her English. Communication requires more than language, and as our language skills improved I became increasingly aware that other components were missing. It takes more than words to cross the distance and scale the barriers between two people spending their lives together. Word nuances, facial expressions, and posture modes deepen the meaning of words and in subtle ways communicate presence or absence of emotional components, which in turn create the elusive and delicate atmosphere of intimate relationships.

As we got over the language hurdles, we had difficulty moving into the shades and tones of emotional exchange, and thence true understanding. I believe it would be fair to say we never achieved that goal. Looking back, I can honestly say I never really understood much about what went on inside Marguerite's head or her heart. I don't think she ever really knew me. Obviously, with five children I'm not speaking in the biblical sense. As I think about it and go one step further, I don't think either of us ever put much effort into knowing the other. I mentioned not being much of a talker. The two of us could be together in the same room or car for hours and hours and never say a word.

Marguerite enjoyed the children when they were babies and cared for them like little girls care for baby dolls. It was her forte. Unfortunately, she tended to keep our youngest child in that role.

•

You may or may not consider this another topic, but I do and so I separate it. The previous segment was about the beginning. Let's get it over with and do the ending.

As I said, the one love of my life was Jane, and I loved her the first time I saw her, yes, immediately. But the behavior was not precipitous this time and the love was not a fantasy. As our relationship developed over a period of time, Jane left her husband, which was long overdue. He was, to say the least, emotionally abusive.

We both lived in the D.C. area. We found an apartment for Jane in Richmond. In a short time, Jane got a job at Thalhimers Department Store, and before long was an assistant buyer. She moved to Richmond because she could file for divorce in Virginia and obtain it within a year's time. I left my house in Bethesda every Tuesday morning about six o'clock and drove to Richmond to see Jane, returning to my office late afternoon. This continued for about eighteen months. And there were other times we took short trips together. After one year, Jane obtained an uncontested divorce.

I went to an attorney in January of 1966 to initiate a divorce with the plan to continue the thriving psychiatric practice I had in the D.C. area. My attorney gave me his card and advised me to ask Marguerite to obtain an attorney who should get in touch with him. I followed his recommendation. By this time, the wall between Marguerite and me was quite obvious within the home, but not to outsiders. As months past, I kept asking her about getting an attorney. She denied having one.

In the American Psychiatric News, I saw an advertisement for the position of Superintendent of the Nevada State Hospital. This opened up the possibility of a Nevada divorce to resolve the stalemate. I flew to Reno, applied, and was accepted with a start date in September.

In preparation for the move, I began taking books and some belongings from my home to my office. With my six year old daughter in the house, that's what I was doing one evening in early August 1966. I answered the door bell and found two policemen come to take me to the Montgomery County Jail. I said I had my daughter in my care, but they assured me her mother was waiting just down at the corner. Well planned!

I spent the night in "the tank" of the county jail on a ne exeat (thou shalt not depart) court order based on the claim I was leaving the state with no provision for my wife or children. Marguerite's attorney had obtained the order on July 4th. I always imagined him playing a few rounds with some judge and then sitting down for a couple of drinks, *like buddies do*. They had been waiting to use it. The next morning my attorney could not procure bail because it was known I was preparing to leave the state. (I had written to my referral sources notifying them of my departure). I could remain in jail three weeks waiting for a hearing (perhaps the same judge) or sign over my five children, three houses, two cars, and everything I owned except my books and clothing plus pay child support and lifetime alimony. The two attorneys came to the jail in the afternoon and Marguerite's attorney, *just by chance*, had all the documents ready for me to sign.

Jane and I left for Nevada three days later. I came to know something about post-traumatic stress. I could not watch a movie showing someone in jail. Called for jury duty about twenty years later I became so anxious being in the court room I was excused. I testified in court several times in Grants Pass, Oregon, but this was as a forensic witness.

•

Enter again Judge Tom in Reno. After we became friends with Tom and his wife, I told him my "court" story. He advised me to continue paying child support but discontinue alimony payments in order to force another hearing on the case. He considered my "jailhouse" agreement was signed "under duress and was unconscionable." I did as he advised and it was not until 1984 a court in Spokane vacated the prior agreement, and the alimony due from 1968 was dismissed. You can be sure I remember that attorney in daily prayers. Since 1964, Marguerite had been managing and collecting money from two of the houses we had jointly owned, and which were rented as apartments and separate rooms. They provided a good income for her. (They had provided my Georgetown tuition and living expenses for family.) By 1984 she had been working at a bank for many years.

Judge Tom was a dear friend but had an annoying habit. He liked to talk and I'm a pretty good listener so we spent pleasant hours together. However, when we still lived in Reno, I would frequently get a phone call about eight o'clock Saturday morning, our morning to sleep in. After my "hello," Tom's voice, "Talk to me, Bob." And silence. He really wanted me just to talk to him. You can't discard a good friend over a few phone calls.

•

Recently I had a phone call from Tara, my first year high school granddaughter. She wanted to interview me for a class.

"What do you think of modern technology and how has it affected your life?"

"Well, I've certainly appreciated having electricity instead of reading by a kerosene lamp, and I am grateful to have a bathroom in the house and running water. There is no spring around here where I could find cold water. Refrigerators are quite useful. It's nice not to have to split wood for heat and cooking. I also appreciate the telephone. It's much simpler and less troublesome than having to send a telegram to get an urgent message to someone. I can use the computer, but apart from that, much of what is familiar to you is a puzzle to me and even a bit scary." How the world has changed in 95 years!

•

Do I write about my first marriage to gain sympathy or to attempt to justify some of my behavior? I have had times of bitterness, anger, and yes, hate. And I've had times of feeling sorry for myself. And I'm aware of times I tried to justify behavior that was not justifiable. I believe all of that is gone now. I appreciate those who understand my loss of Jane, but I don't need sympathy. And as for the rest of my life there is no reason for anyone to feel sympathetic. Life is not always kind or just or easy. The Lord has been good to me. I have no misgivings.

I don't feel a need to justify past behavior. I'm aware of its dimensions. I don't justify it or excuse it or dismiss it. And I am at peace with it. Spiritual writers mention the salutary effect of harsh adversities in life. In the book about Alzheimer's I wrote: "My life is richer and certainly dearer as a result of Jane's illness. It is richer because I now have the opportunity to fill my days and nights with an unselfish love for and attention to the person I most treasure. It is dearer because I am sharply aware of the importance and meaning of my presence in the world."

Living with Jane through her illness stretched me spiritually far beyond what I had ever known or imagined. My faith has been deepened, strengthened, intensified. My religion has been personally modified, or perhaps amended where needed to correspond with my experience. My spiritual practices include scripture reading, daily prayer periods, daily Mass in gratitude for Jane and all God's gifts. My spiritual life is richer and with greater awareness than ever before.

Someone said, "Grief is a portal into soul work."

•

I am aware of what could be a spiritual or perhaps a religious conundrum for some. This is how the knotty issue goes. I pray for Marguerite every day and ask God and Marguerite to forgive me for the harshness, the anger, the lies, the deceit, and the vindictiveness that became part of my behavior toward her. At the same time, I am grateful for our separation, for the outcome. So, from my "bad behavior" came a "great good" in my life. Is there a theologian in the house? It's difficult to feel sorry about anything that contributed to my union with Jane. To sum it up, I assume a person can feel sorry because someone got hurt by what you did even though you would do it again if you had the same reason you had before. Of course, knowing all the facts one could do it differently next time. First step, have a cooperative attorney for Marguerite. So, is my sorrow *real sorrow*? I'm sure God handles such things without my trying to figure it out. I'll leave it up to you to struggle with it all, if you want. It's not a problem for me spiritually and never really was.

If you're thinking about a "good Catholic" getting a divorce and marrying again, well, do not fret. It was never a problem for Jane or me. In Reno and later places where we lived, no one knew details of our situation, so we went regularly to Mass and the sacraments. About twelve years after our Reno divorce and Justice of the Peace wedding, we mentioned our situation to our pastor in Spokane. A couple of weeks later, the Chancellor of the Spokane Diocese called me and asked if we would like to have our first marriages annulled. And it happened. We had our third wedding (to each other that is) with Laura in attendance in the sacristy of St. Aloysius Church. I understand the priest who married us left the ministry and is now married. I pray he has found peace and love.

Our first wedding was in the Catholic Church in Richmond, Virginia. It was probably sometime in the summer or fall of 1965. It was a very private ceremony, no rings, just the two of us present. Who presided? Well, I think God did. "Whom God has joined together." Jane and I stood in the church and said private vows pledging our fidelity to one another. We did not make it an anniversary date, but it was always a memorable occasion. In fact, we never celebrated any of our wedding dates. Every day was a celebration of "us", as Jane used to say.

When Jane first moved to Richmond, she went to see the pastor of that church to become a registered member. He asked some things about her and concluded she must not see me anymore in order to become a member of his parish. She was a second-class Catholic one more time, but it didn't come between her and God. She was always a first-class lady and a first-class Catholic with God, I so believe. And it was not the priest's parish; it was God's parish.

•

I don't think I told you, in Spokane Jane worked as a model for the Nordstrom store and a few others stores throughout the state. The woman who hired her saw her at a church gathering and asked her to model. Jane was doubtful about it but I encouraged her. She was not just a beautiful woman, she was very erect and carried herself well, and she had a smile that would melt a rock. I went to the fashion shows when I could get away from the office. It wasn't Coco Chanel, but they were well done. Jane enjoyed modeling in the window, standing like a manikin for fifteen to twenty minutes. She would wink at the little kids and they were flabbergasted.

After high school, Jane had a four year scholarship to the Moore Institute of Art in Philadelphia. She loved museums but typically sought out the picture that often seemed shunned by other visitors. When she studied a picture she stood at arm's length from it. I asked her why.

"It's where the artist stood when it was painted."

I have a picture she painted in art school and a small picture of pussy willows she did in Reno. I also have the self-portrait she did shortly after we met. It is on the cover of her book.

Jane never really applied her artistic gifts in painting. I never understood her reticence. She would make little sketches on scraps of paper. She bought paints, brushes and all the necessary equipment. Something was blocking her. Was it the unpleasant memory of her first husband's courtship during art school days? She obtained a certificate rather than a degree from art school, primarily because she would skip the degree classes some afternoons to be off with her future husband. Did she feel she had failed herself, her obvious talent?

She was a gifted writer and always carried a little book to write her notes, record her thoughts. She exhibited her artistic talents in the written word. The last chapter in her book, *Before It's Too Late*, contains little notes she wrote during her illness. They are beautiful, painful, heart wrenching, spiritual. They clearly reveal her closeness to God. I wonder if this one relates to her artistic ability.

"I talk to God constantly as I have always done. I have stopped asking 'why?' Shame, guilt, anger, and 'why didn't I do what I had the talent to do?' fill my head! I no longer create. I have trouble being relaxed with anyone but Rob."

Chapter Four:
Don't Poison the Well

Here's an allegory: As the story begins, let me immediately reveal the identity of the components involved. Vantage House is the *well-keeper*. The water is the *care* provided here. We, the residents, use the water to quench our daily thirst, sometimes requiring abundant amounts to satisfy increased needs.

Many of you probably had experiences with wells when you were children. Wells are still used where "city water" is not available. Water-bearing permeable rocks (aquifers) are the source of both wells and springs. Wells are subject to natural and uncontrollable events, which may temporarily either limit the supply of water or provide unsatisfactory water. Excess of calcium and magnesium leached from the rock provides "hard water" which needs to be "softened" with other chemicals. Excess sulfur in water may change the taste and give water a rotten egg odor. Various contaminants from the earth, the pipe, the screens, and the caisson (walls) may need to be corrected. Failure of parts may occur. In short, a number of things can limit availability and/or potability.

What to do if the water fails in some way: contaminants, leaching chemicals, or failing parts? You, of course, would approach those who provide and manage the well. You would clearly and carefully report the problems and provide all pertinent information you might have. Then you would work cooperatively with the managers in their work to correct the deficiencies.

Without precise and continuing communication with the keepers of the well, it is difficult for them to make corrections in the water supply or its delivery.

Wells sometimes develop unusual problems creating a need for extended evaluation and some trial and error experience. All this takes time and perseverance on the part of the well keepers and patience and objectivity on the part of the water users. It sounds so easy, so calm, so generous.

But it doesn't always go so smoothly. Water (care) is important in our daily life, but when the need is markedly increased there is a major impact on the individual. If obtaining the increase of water (care) involves restriction of movement, limitation of activity, change of environment, and separation from friends and familiar settings the loss is keen and cutting. Strong feelings are aroused. Fear, anxiety, and emotional malaise rise quickly and may well prevent one's forming a calm dispassionate view of water availability and quality.

The water (care) normally provides a sense of comfort and security in our daily life. But when there is a "water problem", whether one's own or someone else's, it is unfortunate but natural that tolerance trickles weakly and criticism flows high. Resulting in:

"The water is inadequate!"

"The water is harming people!"

"The water tastes bad!"

"Water quality is being ignored!"

And each time such comments are repeated, in ***our minds*** the water quality worsens. In such a time, it is important to work calmly and positively with the well keepers and not **poison the well.**

+ + + + + + + + + +

Speaking of wells, can you even imagine how creative pioneers were? Unless you grew up in pioneer country, I doubt you can. How can you turn a bubbling spring of water into a refrigerator? First, you dig the ground around the spring a little deeper. Then you put up four water tight sides all around, sides about three feet long that protrude about ten or twelve inches above the water. You cut a notch about two inches deep and three inches wide in the side where the water will flow away from the spring. Then, to catch the water from the box, you join the box to a shallow wooden trough about four feet long and about four inches deep. With another board, you close the end of the trough away from the spring but cut a notch one inch deep and two inches wide. This trough catches the water from the notched spring box and holds it until it overflows into the creek bed just beyond the trough. Then you build a little house over the whole thing. Put on a door. Call it the Spring House. Voila! A self-cleaning refrigerator! Three inches of ice cold running water. Just set the container of butter or eggs or vegetables or milk, whatever in the cold water. Send the youngest kid to the Spring House to get the chilled items for the next meal. And if he has a free hand have him bring a bucket of water to drink, just dip the bucket in the larger open box where the spring bubbles up. Sorry, I thought you might be interested.

•

Besides the articles I wrote for Vantage Views, I've tried my hand at poetry. Perhaps in imitation of my cowboy poet nephew, Jim McAllister. But I'll write about him later. Here are two of mine inspired by the current season:

RESURRECTION
Bare fingered trees reach heavenward and cry
Is it over? I wanted more. I'm too young to die.
The sun through somber clouds makes soft reply
A fresh green dress when winter gray's gone by.

ALLELUIA
The sentinel trees
Whisper soft and low
The season is changing
Please, don't go
The sap is stirring
The days are long
You'll soon be hearing
The ALLELULIA song!

•

Daylight Saving Time has started. The days are finally getting a bit warmer. Our six inches of snow and ice should soon be gone and four weeks from tomorrow is Easter Sunday. Refer back to Chapter One if you're wondering where the time goes.

During my afternoon walk today, I started thinking about Howard. So, I'm going to tell you about him. An interesting view of the human psyche! Howard was a patient of mine many years ago. He doesn't particularly belong in this story, but then, I'm not sure he ever belonged anywhere. On second thought, he does belong here because he was a man I genuinely cared about and knowing him expanded my knowledge of human nature and furthered my education in psychiatry.

I never really got a good history from Howard because he spent most of his 50 minute hours in non-stop streams of acerbic language aimed at almost everyone he ever knew, or so it seemed. I learned he had been in the service and years ago worked at Marshall Fields in Chicago. Abusive language toward all involved. He married late in life to a woman several years his senior. That seemed to be "holy ground" for him, never a harsh word about the woman who perhaps served as the only caregiver he ever had besides me. Howard filled the office with foul, critical, and vindictive comments about the whole world, or at least every part of it he knew. He was never willing to talk about his childhood, but in my imagination I felt like I knew his physically abusive father and his unemotional, distant mother.

To complicate matters, he and a former military buddy went target shooting in some secluded spot about every two weeks. They had a variety of weapons, which Howard described in detail plus how he visualized his assorted current enemies as targets when he pulled the trigger. I felt like a surgeon draining a life-threatening boil each time he came in.

One day he left my office with his usual wake of air stained with the blue streaks of his words. I was doing some welfare evaluations for the Department of Social Security at the time. My next patient was in the waiting room. He was an unshaven, poorly dressed, disheveled individual, possibly deliberately so to impress me of his need for welfare. I was about two minutes into the interview when there was a knock at the office door. I opened.

Howard very quietly asked, "Are you all right?"

Maybe he was doing a dress rehearsal to be my guardian angel someday. Underneath all the wrath was a tender caring man.

One day Howard's rage had reached a new pitch and was for the first time clearly focused in one place. Howard had a veteran's 25% pension. He received a letter from the Department of Veteran's Affairs reducing his pension to 18%.

His smoldering paranoia was loaded and clearly aimed at the veteran's state office in Portland. I told him to be calm (like telling a hurricane not to rustle the leaves) and I would see what I could do. I wrote to the V.A. and explained the danger and how it could be averted. Howard was appeased and forever grateful for the return of his 25% pension.

Howard first became my patient in Grants Pass, Oregon. After five years there, we moved to Spokane, Washington, which was about a nine hour drive from Grants Pass. Howard insisted he continue seeing me. He would not see anyone else. Once a month he and his wife drove to Spokane and stayed overnight. Howard would see me late afternoon on his arrival and first thing next morning before departure. We continued the same "release the venom" exercises.

About one year after we moved, his wife called to cancel the next appointment. Howard had a bad heart (not sure what) and the doctors wanted to operate (not sure why). A couple of weeks later Howard phoned me (first time ever) and talked with me about his condition and the operation. He didn't ask me directly what I thought he should do, but I had the feeling that was why he called. Or perhaps he wanted to say goodbye because he knew he wouldn't see me again. I didn't encourage surgery. I didn't feel I could. Howard needed peace and the world might be safer. His wife called a few days later and told me she came home from the store and found Howard dead on the bed. His first peace in a long time, maybe a lifetime. The volcanic fire was extinguished. You might judge me harshly for not encouraging the surgery. I stand by my decision.

You might wonder why I saw Howard at all. My care for him was not what most people would consider "therapy." But therapists do see patients who *are not going to change*. Are they beyond help? No, not if help includes supporting them in the life they have (difficult as it may be) and helping prevent deterioration. Some physical impairments cannot be remedied and physicians do what they can to minimize the impact of the difficulty. The same is true for some emotional impairments. Persons so impaired are often frustrating to therapists because they make us feel inadequate. Therapists often have an over-reaching need to "fix it." If these patients don't find a therapist who understands the situation and is willing to provide supportive care, the patient may keep changing therapists and with each disappointing involvement become increasingly desperate.

•

When I write about individuals, I recommend you focus on the person I'm writing about rather than on me as writer. "I do not boast." That's not why I write. I see these as portraits of persons who represent humanity, perhaps in exaggerated or distorted form, but nevertheless with thoughts and feelings and experiences, which may call to mind pieces of ourselves: the anger, the tenderness, the desperation, the humor, the loneliness, the sadness, the affection we encounter in ourselves and others. Their emotions will touch you if you open your heart to hear them.

As an addendum to the above, I will tell you one of the mysteries of life that often surprised me in my work. During extended therapy, it usually became clear what had happened in this patient's life to cause the pain, uncertainty, and troubled emotions they experienced. The question that often puzzled me was: How did they manage to live as competently as they had with the harshness and barrenness of their prior existence? I often thought *someone had made a difference*, perhaps a teacher, a neighbor, a coach, or maybe even a classmate had recognized their value in such a meaningful manner they too caught a glimpse of the person they could become.

Winfred Overholser, M.D. was the Superintendent of St. Elizabeth's Hospital for the Insane (the term of the time) in Washington, D.C. He was Superintendent for 25 years ending his career in 1962.

In my judgment, his most famous comment was: "The mentally ill are just like us, only more so." A profound observation. Carry it around for a few years. It will do you good and make you wiser.

•

Since the introduction to this chapter is about "Poisoning the Well," perhaps this is a fitting time to discuss my tenure in Nevada. The job was a great fit for me and a wonderful experience. I gave as a reference Frank Braceland who was and had been for years the Superintendent of the prestigious Institute of Living in Hartford.

An excerpt from his letter: "You asked if Dr. McAllister would make a good superintendent. Well, I don't know what makes a good superintendent, and I didn't know if I would be a good superintendent when I took the position at the Institute of Living." Frank had a wonderfully gentle way of being direct.

For the first three or four months in Reno, I got "the lay of the land." Then I terminated a psychiatrist who was being paid fulltime and who drove from California Tuesday afternoon and went home Thursday afternoon. I also terminated a psychiatrist who was drunk on night call. That was appealed to the Nevada State Personnel Board and my decision was upheld about one year later. The hospital internist was displeased when I told him he actually had to be at the hospital when he was scheduled to be on duty. He quit after a short time.

Dana Farnsworth, a psychiatrist friend from Harvard, told me once, "To be a good administrator, you have to have the ability to inflict pain."

I discovered the harsh truth of it in the aftermath of an inept predecessor.

Jane and I moved to Nevada in September. She had her own apartment for a month and then quietly moved into the superintendent's house on hospital grounds. It took almost three months for me to get a Reno divorce. After the divorce, to avoid Reno press, we were quietly married by a Justice of the Peace in Truckee, California.

Some of those who became disenchanted with or who were terminated from the hospital put a flyer on all car windows in downtown Reno the following Easter Sunday. It was titled: **Nevada's Esteemed Adulterer**. Large print heading with a full page of my sins and sordid depravities. The flyer accused me in colorful description of being: (1) An adulterer (which almost became the least of my sins because I was also), (2) a papist (and likely to spread all kinds of evil right out of Rome), and (3) a communist (with a penchant for various crimes to overthrow the government). Each member of the legislature had received a copy of the page. The flyer was on our windshield as we left Easter Sunday Mass at the Reno Cathedral.

Needless to say Jane and I were devastated and anticipated being asked to leave my position. I served "at the pleasure of the governor." Paul Laxalt was governor; he later became State Senator, and then Chairman of the Republican Party for several years. Dr. Otto Ravenholt, my boss, lived in Las Vegas. I phoned him shortly after we got home from Mass.

His response, "I'll come up this afternoon and we'll talk."

He flew up and came to the house for dinner. He had met Jane and had been to dinner once or twice before. After a lengthy discussion Otto made a decision about how the matter would be handled.

Monday morning at our usual administrative staff meeting of about ten people, we had our nursing and incident reports. After the reports were completed and discussed, I gave a copy of the flyer to my business manager and asked him to read it to the group after I left the room. (This was my decision, not part of Otto's plan).

I drove directly to Carson City to meet Otto. The state legislature was in joint session that morning. After the session opened, Otto introduced me to the assembly and praised me for my work. His comments could be summarized by the bible story, "He who is without sin cast the first stone." Slander was not to be tolerated in Nevada and the entire body said so by giving me a big round of applause. The matter was ended. It was never addressed by anyone in my presence and I believe the story died that day at the hospital.

There was one exception. Monsignor Regini, pastor at the Cathedral and the one who said the Easter Mass during the scarlet letter droppings, called me Easter afternoon and asked us to come to the same Mass the following Sunday. His homily was equally as direct as Otto's had been and with the same gospel story.

There was one small benefit from the whole affair. That Monday morning before the legislature convened I met the chairman of the finance committee. He was concerned about a sliver in his finger. I took it out for him with a pin. A year or so later, we got an increase in the hospital budget. I think my minor surgery helped our cause.

•

The Reno job was very challenging and very rewarding, although financially limited. We did have a house on the grounds with all utilities and the crew to respond to our needs. The experience was broad; staff was loyal, positive, and competent. Opportunities to stretch some boundaries, make some improvements were available. We got the hospital accredited by Medicare, bringing in more revenue. I wrote a grant request and obtained a National Institute of Mental Health (NIMH) grant for staff education. Instead of choosing a few staff and paying for them to attend educational opportunities elsewhere, we brought some of the most prominent men in the psychiatric world to Reno for two day presentations. We invited mental health professionals in the Reno area to come to the lectures. It was good publicity for the hospital.

As I think of it, "the most prominent men" sounds sexually biased. This was the 60's. If there were any women psychiatrists at that time, I had never heard of them. There was one woman in my class at Georgetown, but none in my residency program.

When these out of town lecturers came, we had a small reception at the Superintendent's House inviting our professional staff, Otto, and Paul Laxalt.

Laxalt came on several occasions. Jane was always a remarkably welcoming and gracious hostess. Her background in Philadelphia had been marked with poverty. Her mother and stepfather worked in local hosiery mills and Jane joined them at age fourteen (war time). In spite of her limited experience, her natural endowment of warmth and kindness put everyone at ease during these receptions. On Christmas Day, we always had an "open house" and invited all hospital staff to come by for a bit of holiday cheer.

Ours was the only psychiatric hospital in Nevada. When residents in Las Vegas were committed for care they were housed in the local jail until the sheriff's van was available once a week to transport them north to Reno. They arrived in hand-cuffs and foot shackles after the six hour trip. Not a very good introduction to mental health care. Psychiatric care was severely limited in Las Vegas. The two available psychiatrists charged exorbitant fees. In those days, it was cheaper to fly to and from Los Angeles and visit a psychiatrist there.

We requested and obtained another grant from NIMH to build and open in Las Vegas the first Comprehensive Mental Health Center in the western region of the U.S. Jane, who had an innate sense of design and proportion, worked closely with the architect in some of the decisions involved in the buildings and their furnishings. As a result of the new Center, psychiatric patients no longer spent time in jail in Las Vegas and the sheriff's transportation to Reno was no longer needed. CMHC's were the forward looking product of the Kennedy presidency back in 1963 and a tremendous asset in the care of the mentally ill.

After my first two years in Reno, the Director of the State Mental Health and Mental Retardation Program resigned. Paul Laxalt asked me to take on the additional responsibility. The new post required my visiting Las Vegas from time to time. These trips as well as the nearness of Reno to Lake Tahoe provided Jane and me the opportunity to see performances of the brightest stars of Broadway and Hollywood. Reno was a fantastic place to live and an enriching experience for both of us.

•

You might wonder how I knew these nationally prominent psychiatrists. From 1964 to 1973 I had the privilege of being on the faculty of the Pastoral Mental Health Institute at St. John's University in Collegeville, Minnesota.

The Institute provided one week of mental health training for ministers of all faiths. There were six faculty members each week and three separate weekly sessions. Most of the faculty members were distinguished psychiatrists teaching in prominent universities or administering outstanding hospitals. I was markedly out-classed. Most of them had been friends with each other for years (ex-Navy psychiatrists). I was again an outsider, but they were warm and gracious to me. It was one of the golden opportunities of my life and most rewarding to meet and discuss topics of faith and mental health with my fellow psychiatrists as well as attending clergy.

•

Tom Craven, Frank Braceland, Paul Laxalt, and Otto Ravenholt were four men in my life to whom I owe a great deal. Each was supportive in my time of need and I benefitted from their confidence. Apart from their influence in my life, I admired their strength, their competence, and their compassion. Each is remembered daily in prayer. The four of them are deceased.

Otto was a gifted administrator. He was insightful, loyal, wise and creative (and politically astute) in his decisions. I inherited a business manager at the hospital who was doing an unsatisfactory job. After observing the man's incompetence for several months, I spoke to Otto about him and gave him the details. To terminate a state employee, we had to go through a lengthy process of documenting, counseling, documenting another episode, counseling, and on to a third episode before we could terminate.

Otto's solution: "Let's promote him."

I was dumbfounded.

Otto explained, "I'll give him a job in Carson City (state capital in case you don't remember) where he won't get in anyone's way and won't do any damage."

It worked for me. I replaced him with a truly excellent business manager.

The first time I met Otto he came to the hospital to get acquainted. It was quite comfortable to sit and talk with him in my office. We were obviously compatible. I asked if he would like to come to dinner at my house. He agreed. I called Jane to let her know. She was pleased and welcomed him with her usual warmth, charm, and good cooking. Otto told me later he always liked to meet the partner of anyone who worked for him. He said the relationship between the two told him a great deal. He and Jane maintained a harmonious relationship. Many years later he visited us in Spokane.

I learned something from Otto and had need of it soon after the episode with my business manager. My personal secretary had a nephew who consulted at the hospital. He was a teaching psychologist at the University of Nevada, the psychologist I previously mentioned with the Lizzie Borden report. I discovered he was not consistently at the hospital during the hours he entered on his time card. I knew the Psychology Department Chairman, but rather than call I put my complaint in a letter. My secretary typed it and gave it to me with an envelope for mailing. For no particular reason and unintentionally, I put the letter in my desk and left it there for a few days. A couple of days after the letter was typed, I got a call from the Chairman asking what the problem was with so-and-so. Clearly my secretary had given the information to her nephew who apparently went to his Chairman to defend himself.

It would have been impossible to terminate the secretary. She was heart and soul Nevadan, friend of politicians and big-wigs. So, I promoted her. At this time, I needed a new assistant for the Mental Retardation branch of my job. I offered the job to a man I knew well and trusted, but I told him my secretary went with his promotion. I admit, I got some satisfaction the morning I walked into my office and said to my secretary, "Genevieve, take your coat and your purse and leave the office. You are transferred to another position." Within a year of her transfer, Genevieve was hospitalized a sort time and died. She is in my prayers.

The man I promoted to the job was an interesting fellow. He was blind from birth. He married the woman who was his "reader" in college. They were a delightful couple and our good friends. Jack collected and repaired old clocks. Their house was full of his clocks, all running. If they had all been synchronized, I believe the house may have rocked a bit with their ticking. Since it didn't, I presume while some of them ticked, the others "tocked" as counterbalance. The couple visited us in our house and Jack was always there for hospital receptions. He knew every piece of furniture in our living room and advised me that one of the tables had a loose nail in a piece of trim. Although totally blind, he *saw* with touch and keen awareness much that others never saw. I might say he was an insightful man.

As I write about these people, I recall the significance they had in my life and what a major learning experience it was for me to interact with them in such direct and meaningful ways. Although I was in my late 40's I was relatively naïve in the complexities of a world that required negotiation, appeasement, creative and sometimes harsh decisions that deeply affected the lives of others.

Chapter Five:
Not Shangri-La After All

In the 1933 James Hilton novel, *Lost Horizon*, people lived beyond their normal lifespan and aged very slowly in the mystical land of Shangri-La.

As one moves through the halls and common rooms of Vantage House and notices residents actively engaged in a variety of programs throughout the day and evening, one might have the thought: "This is a retirement community for the elderly. Have these people discovered a fantasyland where aging is delayed, for surely they do not appear aged. They are so active! They seem so involved! So engaged! So responsive to life! Is this perhaps some idyllic place where harmony and happiness surround?"

All needs were provided for in the storybook land of Shangri-La. And so it seems to be here at Vantage House. Is it possible we are lulled into the belief we have found an adult version of Never-Never Land? Life in Vantage House is a bit seductive. It entices us to imagine we have escaped the world of adult responsibilities because "staff" takes care of the many items which are the anticipated burden of these elder years.

If something is broken, we call Buildings Services. If there is snow in winter, it is cleared away before we've decided whether or not to leave the building. Transportation Services take us to five or six different places to buy groceries, also to restaurants, the Columbia Mall, the Bank, concerts, plays, and special events. Environmental Services come once a week to provide fresh linens and to tidy up the apartment. Dining Services provide a delicious variety of foods in the dining room and the café leaving us uncertain what to choose from so many dishes we like.

Life Enrichment Services expand our lives and our interests with widely diversified programs in-house and in several other venues including museums and attractions in the Greater Baltimore-Washington area. Our days and evenings are luxuriant with opportunities to attend lectures, play pool, bridge, mahjong, scrabble, bingo, and to watch movies, old and new. Lecture topics include the arts, history, current affairs, health, travel, and other topics. Day programs offer ceramics class, mixed media art class, knitting, crocheting, book discussion and Wii games. Day and evening musical programs bring entertainers in classical, jazz, ragtime, and the oldies. The Wellness Center strives to minimize any health limitations which may intrude in our golden, vaporous world. Care is available in the Wellness Center for those minor ailments that disturb our serenity and the way of life we expect magically to maintain. More serious health problems receive needed attention and care in the Health Center.

To enhance this pursuit of lasting good health and well-being, the Fitness Center staff offers individual attention and guidance in the use of equipment in the exercise room. To continue and possibly enhance our physical and mental health, they offer a medley of exercise classes: muscle toning, balance class, lower back and abdominal workout, keep moving aerobics, yoga movements, cardio kickboxing, balance class, Tai Chi, and Tai Chi Chih.

Add to all this, Concierge and Security Services available 24 hours a day to respond to immediate needs or problems and Social Services staff to help us find our way in this diverse but remarkably harmonious world.

Is it not surprising if on occasion one drifts off into a mirage of Shangri-La? If it happens now and then, it is not for long! The reality of mortality is close at hand. There are reminders! Awareness our memory is not as functional as it used to be. Discovering our balance has lost some accuracy and our hearing some acuity. Aches and pains no longer dismissed as quickly and easily as in the past. The friend last week who was noticeably failing and now no longer comes to the dining room. The black bordered card on the bulletin board announcing a permanent departure. A sense of sadness and loss vaguely haunts our idle moments. A quiet, fleeting wish for Shangri-La.

+ + + + + + + + +

One Sunday afternoon in Reno, Jane and I decided to go to a Vacation Vehicle Show at the Fairgrounds. As I think about this, I realize Jane and I were equally precipitous in some of the joint decisions we made, especially the important ones. Every house we bought was decided almost at first sight although we did look at others. The only decision that didn't turn out great was the one I made to move to Maine, a decision with which Jane was not in full agreement. Yet that one also turned out well in the long run. And the "long run" is really what life is all about. I guess the "long stop" is the real measure of life.

That particular Sunday afternoon we bought a Chevrolet truck with an over-cab camper. We had no plan to purchase anything. "No, just looking, thanks." The vehicle became an important part of our life. We called the camper "Tolivar," from our favorite Roger Miller song, "We Called Our Love Tolivar."

On weekends we camped just outside Reno in the Sierra Nevada's overlooking Lake Tahoe. We went to Disneyland in it, Collegeville, MN, Victoria, B.C., Las Vegas, and on a week's vacation to the Oregon coast. On the latter trip, we camped near Tillamook. Jane was always in love with the ocean, and the Oregon coast is strikingly beautiful. In her enamored state, Jane talked of us buying a house somewhere there.

On the way back to Reno, we looked at a few. We found one in Nesika Beach, a few miles north of Gold Beach, a little two bedroom waterfront on a cliff about fifty feet up from the ocean. $20,000—just short of a year's pay. We decided to buy it. I had no checkbook, no credit card, and not much cash left. We paid $20 down and signed the contract. I sent the remainder of the down payment after our eight hour drive back to Reno. That became our vacation home for about two years in spite of the long drive. Actually, the property had two lots; the house was on the inland lot.

It sounds ridiculous to say, "We bought a house," when my annual salary was approximately $22,000. But when people say, "I bought a house," it usually refers to the down payment. One should say, "I bought a mortgage." During our years together, we eventually bought eight houses but never *owned* one.

•

The title of this chapter mentions Shangri-La. Well, Reno was not Shangri-La after all, because of the "wicked witch" if I may mingle fairytale with fiction. I guess fairytales are also fiction. If you believe fairytales are true, perhaps you should make an appointment with me. But I warn you, I may not have many hours still available.

Paul Laxalt lost reelection, but later was elected to the U.S. Senate. The newly elected Governor Callahan was a democrat and an Irish Catholic. I never met him. I must say I didn't care for the man. Why? You know, just one of those things. Instinct, his looks, a feeling, the way he spoke? Truly, I don't know why, but I knew I didn't like him for some reason I could never clarify for myself.

Otto Ravenholt was back in Vegas and Callahan appointed Roger Troundy, another Catholic, as my new boss. "Catholic" shouldn't matter one way or the other. Or at least I didn't think so at the time. Several weeks of the new regime went by. The hospital was running smoothly. No problems. Eight o'clock one morning I walked the thirty or forty yards from my front door to the hospital. "Good morning," I said to the switchboard operator just inside the front door.

As I walked by, she said, "Mr. Troundy was here at six o'clock this morning and asked to have a tour of the hospital. One of the nursing staff took him around."

That was a bit of a surprise.

Two or three additional weeks went by and no one got in touch with me from Carson City. I was puzzled, suspicious. Why six a.m.? Why no contact? I knew Roger well. We spent time with him in a church group from our parish. Something brewing? Jane and I talked about my resigning before I might be terminated at the pleasure of the governor. I wasn't keen about working for Callahan anyway.

We considered staying in Reno and my opening a private practice there, but my heart, and at least half my mind, would have stayed at the hospital. We agreed to move. The question "where" was already settled, to Southern Oregon near the beach house of course.

I took some time off and we went to Oregon. Gold Beach was too small for a psychiatric practice. Grants Pass, a three hour drive inland, was a good size town and had a Mental Health Clinic. No psychiatrists in town. I got a half-time job working at the clinic. We always drove through Grants Pass on previous trips to Gold Beach vacations (at the Nesika Beach house). On one of those previous trips, we drove around Grants Pass just looking. Jane saw a stately looking three story house and said if we ever moved to Grants Pass that was the house she wanted. On this trip it was for sale. We bought it of course, but we did look (feebly) at a couple of others.

Returning to Reno, we made our plans to move. We had an annual hospital staff talent show scheduled in mid-October. I announced my resignation at the end of the show. Many went home with tears in their eyes, including Jane and me. I informed the press the following morning and then sent my letter to Callahan with a month's notice. There was no reply, which did not surprise me.

I have no doubt he was going to terminate me. I'm reasonably sure I'm not just being paranoid. And I have always asked myself, "Why?" Was he a democrat getting rid of republican appointees? But I had been appointed by a democrat governor prior to Laxalt taking office. Was it because of the *Easter letter* and his Catholic faith got the better of his judgment? I didn't know him, but I had a dislike. Maybe he felt the same way about me for the same "no reason."

Just today as I was walking, another possibility came to mind for the first time. Did he owe someone a special favor, someone who had supported him financially or in some other way individuals arrange for politicians to owe them? The psychiatrist I fired? The internist who quit over his required attendance? Genevieve's psychologist nephew? Or one of her powerful and mighty friends? I'll never know. And at this point in time, I couldn't care less.

We moved to Grants Pass just prior to Thanksgiving 1971 and closed the door on the first chapter of our wonderful life together.

•

Christian churches are recognizing the end of Lent. The feeling of pain, of separation, of suffering and death permeate the words and actions of the services and leave their shadow on our minds and hearts. Then there is the transcendent joy of Easter morning. We are in a religious season replete with imagery.

My life has become some sort of "conversion experience" in which I embrace it as one interlocking observation no longer separated by "when" or "where" but currently held as one blended entirety. Scenes, events, experiences, feelings from earlier times easily cross to the present through the mist of artificial boundaries.

Easter is the feast of resurrection which we celebrate in each funeral that takes place. Of course, I think of Jane's funeral, my Mom's, my Dad's and other loved ones. The only sibling's funeral I was available to go to was my brother Jim when I was eight years old. He died of a ruptured appendix in the days before penicillin. Another brother is buried in a WWII military cemetery in the Philippines. When my closest and dearest brother, Don, died, I could not go because of Jane's Alzheimer's. I would not leave her alone.

•

The risen Lord brings peace and love. There is no difficulty in believing, no, in *knowing* that Jesus is risen. Why can't I have the same belief, the same surety that Jane is risen? We talk and hear others talk about the risen Lord. There is ample evidence in the scriptures. We talk with others about the fact almost as if Jesus were standing beside us. But no one talks about Jane that way. We only speak of *the dead person, the dead Jane*. No one refers to her as if she were truly alive. Of course she has not walked on this earth again or been seen by others since her death.

I talk to Jane about everything, what I'm going to do, what I just did, and then I tell her I know she knows all that or at least I assume she does. She must know what's in my emails, to whom I just talked on the telephone, with whom I had dinner, whom I saw at Mass. Sometimes I tell her what day it is or what time I will be back when I leave the apartment. But time and days must be meaningless in Heaven. Strangely enough, time and days had become meaningless to Jane years *before* she died. Somewhere in St. Paul's writings (I think it's his), he speaks of shedding our worldly self before we are heaven bound. I sometimes wonder if Alzheimer's patients have a head start, so to speak, on the road to heaven. They shed much of themselves unwittingly though unwillingly during the illness.

•

This might be a place to write about the life I enjoyed in the seminary and why I walked away from it all. Again I must clarify. I didn't walk away from my spirituality, my faith or my religion. I walked away from the path that led to the priesthood.

There have been situations in life where I didn't feel I fit in well. The seminary was surely one of the most contented and serene situations of my entire life. It was a "good fit." It was peaceful, prayerful, and filled with a sense of high purpose. It continued my love of learning and fed my need for order and routine. There was a grand sense of fellowship, all of us about the same age sharing the path to a life of service for the Lord and His people. We were close friends sharing the same experience, friends with whom I remained in contact for years. Another significant similarity was our common socio-economic background. No one came from a big city or a wealthy family (or even well-to-do). Those two last mentioned factors have been more significant for me in my present situation than I formerly realized. Some days it's easy to feel I don't belong. I identify strongly with Montana and my cowboy years.

Seminary routines were inflexible. Everything was on a schedule—classes, meals, prayer time, recreation time, hours of silence, bedtime and rising time. No visiting in another's room. Visitors one Sunday a month, relatives only. No newspapers, radios, or telephones. Mail opened and probably checked for propriety. It was a cookie-cutter existence, the same expectation for each finished product. Individuality was not fostered.

St. Edward's Seminary was located on a wooded hill above Lake Washington just outside Seattle. It was a beautiful location and the property included a broad lake front. As I recall, there were no classes on Wednesday and Saturday afternoons. Three of us regularly walked on the nearby highway picking and eating abundant blackberries in season and also picking up discarded bottles. Later, we took the bottles to the lake, threw them into the water, and then threw rocks to break them. It became a war game. The bottles were Japanese ships and the rocks were planes sinking them. Sounds more like a bunch of teenagers. That's about as close to the war as we came.

Around Christmas time of my second year, I began to think about leaving the seminary. I mentioned in a prior chapter about people doing things and not knowing why they do them, (e.g. the boy who shot his mother). Well, to some this may have seemed almost as serious as shooting your mother. It certainly had lifetime consequences. We each had a priest as our spiritual director. My director, Father Jim Brennan, was quite surprised with my decision, but to his credit, he did not try to talk me out of it or dissuade me in any way. He did ask me to stay until June, the end of the following semester, to think it over a little longer. I agreed. It was a wise recommendation. It helped me become more certain of a major decision. In retrospect, I might say there were a couple of other decisions in life on which I could well have used the same approach.

Many years later when Jane and I lived in Baltimore, I contacted Father Brennan who was then retired and living in the area in housing for retired priests. He came to visit Jane and me several times and on one occasion took me to an Orioles ballgame. I went to confession to him one more time before I had surgery for prostate cancer.

•

Another sidebar please. I had many Catholic priests and sisters as patients during my days of private practice. A good number of them were unhappy in their choice of religious life. When we talked about their years of training many of them told me about significant doubts they had prior to the solemn profession of vows. The response of their spiritual director to their doubts was often something like this: "Everyone gets doubts along the way and you must try to discount these doubts as temptations of the devil to keep you from giving your life to God and serving God and God's people." Unfortunately, if the doubt had been discussed, opened, and explored an unhappy conflicted life might have been avoided.

•

I could just go on to another subject and ignore the question on the table: Why did I decide to leave the seminary? The topic may not interest you, although you may be a little curious. It leaves me curious because I can't recall my precise thinking at the time. Well, I met a girl in Dubuque during my senior year of college. I only knew her a few months. We used to visit on her doorstep. Never really "went on a date." Eileen was still in my mind. But that doesn't really answer the question. I think I felt the need for female companionship and somehow my life would not be complete otherwise. At the time, that was not verbalized even to myself. It just seemed to be *something my heart was telling me to do*. I had the mental qualifications, probably the personal qualifications, to be a priest, but I honestly believe I would have eventually found it to be an extremely lonely life. The end point? An expression from ranch life comes to mind: sooner or later I would have kicked over the traces.

One might raise the question of celibacy. Yes, if celibacy had not been a requirement, I would probably be a priest today. But then, I would never have met Jane, and I can't imagine life without her. Celibacy or no celibacy, I thank God every day for the decision to leave the seminary.

•

For most of us, the Easter season brings to mind Easter eggs and the joy of children in the hunt. The Easter egg hunt contains the elements of something precious, something lost, something hidden, a great surprise, and a joyful find. The egg of course is a symbol of new life. The egg seekers are the women and men at the tomb seeking Jesus.

At Eastertime, I have my own story of the *God of the Easter Eggs*. I believe when God created the world God hid all things yet to be discovered. All the great and wonderful so-called inventions and scientific discoveries brought forth by the women and men of science and learning are simply the Easter eggs God left to be found. No one really invents anything. They don't discover it, they uncover it and bring it out of hiding.

"There is nothing new under the sun."

•

There is a current news story about an airplane that crashed into the mountains in southern France. Sixteen school children and a total of 150 passengers and crew met sudden death. Citizens of several countries were involved in the disaster. People all over the world mourned the tragedy.

When young people, especially babies, die I always think about the parable of the workers in the vineyard. The parable says those who begin work late in the day receive the same pay as those who began working at the beginning of the day.

It seems to me the parable applies in the airplane crash and similar situations only in a sort of reverse manner. The young come to work in the vineyard, but they are relieved of their task early in the day, sometimes in the first few hours, other times in the first few years. Others labor in the vineyard fifty, eighty, a hundred years and receive the same reward any baby or younger person receives. Some have "worked" a few days, others a hundred years. The reward is the same for all. I'm assuming all are "in the state of grace" as the Catholic Church might say. I would replace those words with "on good terms with God." Most certainly the infants and young are. Finally, I always remind myself a heavenly reward is so complete, so encompassing there is nothing else to want. So, what if I have worked 95 years! Or more!

I do not make light of the death of anyone in these remarks. But I would highlight that primarily we are mourning our loss. We may speak of the deceased's loss of a future, a career they started, children they have or planned on having, or the joy of living. In reality, none of that compares to what they have gained.

•

After leaving the seminary in June 1943, I volunteered for the service and ended up an infantryman in Patton's Third Army. I mention this here because it occurs to me that my feelings about the military were undoubtedly colored by the contrast between seminary life and service life. Although both were highly structured, a marked disparity was certainly present. Leaving the seminary was like leaving home: a safe, nurturing, peace-filled, spiritual, and embracing environment. Boot camp was as great a contrast as anyone could possibly imagine. There is no need for descriptive details.

By the way, no one in my family grieved my leaving the seminary, at least as far as I knew. I think they had been pleased when I entered the seminary although nothing much was ever said about it. During my adolescent years, my mother often said I should be a doctor. And so it happened.

Chapter Six:
The Bottom Line

This phrase usually refers to our monetary balance, our financial worth. Rich, poor, or middleclass, the value and use of money has, in one way or another, forced itself into our lives. How much will it cost? What's it worth? Will it last? Is it really worth it? Can I afford it? Should I get it? Do I need it? We have all gone through this labyrinth of thought, sometimes superficially for minor items, sometimes deceptively because our decision was already made, and sometimes seriously with research and time. Even in retirement, we continue to watch the bottom line. With a relatively fixed income and haunting uncertainty about needs of the future, the bottom line remains important.

But let's for a moment transfer this "bottom line" concept to other life treasures: intellect, physical health, emotions, or one might say mind, body, and spirit. Have we appreciated their presence and their worth? Have we acknowledged their value to us and to others? Have we spent these resources wisely and well? Are the accounts still open and how are they doing? Do we still make deposits or only withdrawals?

The account of mind (intelligence) was determined primarily by heredity, but access to the account and its value became apparent in our educational years. Assets grew proportionally to our investment in educational opportunities and our own personal learning pursuits. For most of us, the account remains open for additional deposits as we peruse the books, newspapers and magazines in the extensive library at Vantage House, attend the various lectures and programs in the weekly schedule of events, or engage in meal time or free time conversation with peers. If we ignore opportunities to maintain a healthy account balance, we will find the regular withdrawals made by *passive* everyday living are slowly depleting the account. If you just leave your money in the bank, over time its true value lessens. If your mind is idle, inactivity gradually drains the asset.

Body, represented by physical health, is a highly valued treasure throughout life and especially in later years. As with mind, ancestry determines much of the initial deposit for this account. Further investment comes primarily from an active life, a healthy diet and regular exercise. Neglecting these quickly depletes even a healthy start-up fund. The broad variety of healthy choices in the Vantage House dining room and availability of exercise equipment and classes provide opportunities to grow our account. Illness and injurious accidents may draw heavily and abruptly on our health account and make increasing demands over subsequent years. Limitation of movement, reduction of sensory acuity, and various painful and debilitating disorders may bring individuals to the verge of bodily bankruptcy. The situation may require "falling back on other resources," primarily those treasures of mind and spirit, which may assist a person in maintaining optimum physical function in spite of serious limitations.

The last of our non-monetary, non-tangible treasures now comes to the fore. What is this *spirit*, these *emotions* poets write about, psychologists study, philosophers describe, and people live? We are familiar with the capriciousness of these forces which seem to have a life of their own as they invade our relationships, stain our days, and color our activities. Troublesome as they can sometimes be, they provide much of the capital that keeps us "spending ourselves" in the difficult times, the dreary, overwhelming, lonely, despairing times when our body and mind accounts seem "broke." They comprise the "spirit" that disallows permanent retreat to the dark corners of life.

How does one maintain a profitable reserve of spirit? Imagine a pool of emotional forces. Ancient Greeks and Romans believed four humours (bodily fluids) comprised our moods and feelings. The secret of maintaining a healthy spirit-pool is to spend the capital in a manner that brings return. Investing kindness, love, gentleness, and generosity returns double dividends. It enlarges our inner sense of personal worth and it provides good to another. Anger, hostility, prejudice are also in the pool of spirit. To express them is like writing bad checks, they do double damage. Recipients are demeaned and the writer has devalued self.

Life presents a variety of treasures. Be grateful for them. Be generous with them. The principal grows in the sharing.

+ + + + + + + + + +

Frank Braceland (my Reno reference) didn't know what an administrator needed to be a good administrator. I didn't know either, but I think I became a good administrator. It was in the doing that I learned. I never saw myself as "in charge", but rather as someone who worked with the other employees to do what needed to be done. I listened to them, watched them, and got to know them not just from afar, but by seeing them, talking to them. It is probably not surprising I often took my lunch and went to the shop to eat with the maintenance crew. I felt at home with them. Slim, Mitch, Charlie, Frank and Oscar: their names are still with me and my prayers. They also took care of needs in our house and yard, so Jane knew them too.

One day Charlie was fixing something in the overhead crawl space. The doorbell rang, Jane went, no one there. Doorbell again. After three or four times, Charlie playfully told her he was connecting the wires off and on in the attic. She was comfortable with the crew, and they with her. Charlie had a glass eye and he would occasionally take it out with comment to Jane:

"I'll keep my eye on that."

Silly stories, right? Not really of value or importance. Well, what do you usually collect from the past that will make you happy later? Jewelry, fine clothes? How about watches, cars, menus of fine restaurants, or souvenirs of cruises, antiques? We collected, not just friends, but people we cared about, had a bond with, enjoyed being with, and when they were gone from our lives, we still remembered them. Stories bring back those lost or left behind. It isn't the face, the facts, or even the name you will remember when you're really old. It's the story!

•

Jane collected a wide variety of things. Never fine clothes, never expensive jewelry. I bought her gold earrings for her birthday in the late 80's. She insisted I take them back. She gathered a few fine antiques, not because they were antiques, but because they reached out and touched her soul. If we walked down an alley, she might find something in someone's trash she "needed." Ordinary little rocks were often not so ordinary for her and they came home with us. On the Oregon coast, we had driftwood all over the house and yard. I have two of her windows (actually cabinet doors) with five lights in each hanging on my wall. A small piece of cement with some red paint (torn off a curb by a snowplow) is a treasure we found at the mall. Now it sits by her cinerarium.

As Jane's memory of friends faded and we could no longer comfortably reminisce about them, I think she turned more to the tangible memories of "her things." I would see her caressing pieces of furniture, rubbing and feeling them with her lovely loving hands. She increasingly worried about what would happen to "her things" after her death. I brought them with me when I moved to a smaller apartment. I planned to get an antique dealer to look at them with the idea of finding a buyer for them after my death. None of our "baby boomer" children have an interest or an "eye" for any of them. One day, not long ago, I decided quite suddenly, but clearly, almost as if someone whispered it in my ear, to give the treasured pieces to our treasured (and more traditional) friends from church. See how some treasures really do multiply. I know the decision pleases Jane.

One of Jane's most remarkable "finds" was a number of windows being replaced in an apartment complex near our house in Baltimore. She asked the foreman if she could have some of the old windows.

His response: "How many do you want?"

Jane replied, "I'll get back to you." We had a large screened porch on the back of our Baltimore house. We needed about ten windows to enclose it. The foreman delivered them without charge. I enclosed the porch, adding a new door with glass. Lo, a highly useable sunroom!

•

The fix-it-yourself life on the ranch was a training ground for me. I learned to use all the available tools. I was essentially "tool-less" through seminary days, service time, and the beginning of my graduate studies. My doctorate at Catholic University was obtained using the G.I. Education Bill. That source was exhausted by the time I went to Georgetown Medical School. I had the good fortune to buy (for a minimum down payment) two adjoining row houses in a good D.C. location. With Marguerite and our two children, we moved into one, using the first floor and attic for ourselves. We rented four rooms on the second floor plus the basement. I converted the basement and two adjoining rooms on second floor into two efficiency apartments. The second house was made into furnished rooms and apartments. I installed electric wiring, plumbing, and gas stoves. I built closets and installed doors and windows as needed. How did I know how to do all this? With the skills I learned as a boy and the pioneer spirit of initiative and daring, I learned how in the doing. Income from the two houses and several other odd jobs provided for us and paid my way through medical school.

I somehow got hooked up with a marketing firm in Chicago. They sent me consumer surveys to do, for example, logos for products or companies. The current red "S" logo for Safeway is one I remember because it was chosen then and is still around. I had other jobs here and there. I worked in Real Estate, even helped put the Sunday newspapers together at the Washington Post.

•

I want to write more about my father. He was an old-fashioned Irish Catholic, honest as could be, a good neighbor, kept up his part of the fence. Cattle did not just roam the land. We had barbed wire fences. If it was a fence between you and a neighbor, you were responsible for the right half. Of course, if the neighbor did not maintain his half, then his cattle might be grazing in your pasture or yours in his. Even worse, his bull might get in with your cows causing three potential problems: his bulls might breed your cows in the wrong season or the bull might be of a breed you did not want mixed into your herd. Thirdly, if your own bulls were available, there might be a real bull fight with no matadors to distract them, only additional barbed wire fences to be torn down by two angry bulls. Robert Frost was so right: "Good fences make good neighbors."

As I said before, Dad was a quiet man and unfortunately I can't say I knew him well, at least not directly. I always envied my brother Don, five years my senior who remained on the ranch all his life. Later in life, Don wrote a booklet about the family, *Lives and Legacies*. He was deservedly my father's favorite and in my parents' age of poor health, Don and his wife Helen took care of Dad and Mom. Dad had a severe stroke, was hemiplegic, and lost coherent speech. They took care of him in their house on the ranch. Helen, not a nurse, was his nurse. Don carried him to the table for his meals and helped him eat. Mom was in the hospital when Dad died and she followed him in death shortly afterwards.

After my parents died, Helen developed Parkinson's disease and Don took care of her for eight years or more. Don needed his hips replaced. He had them both done at the same time so he could get home to Helen. While Don was still recuperating, he tried riding his horse. It didn't go too well. When he mentioned it to his doctor, the doctor asked him why he did a dumb thing like that.

Don's reply: "Well, you didn't tell me not to." Cowboy logic! Too bad the horse wasn't smart enough not to let him mount.

Don's caring for our parents and then his wife for so many years was an inspiration to me during the time of Jane's Alzheimer's. Present or absent, he was always a steady star in my life.

My writing wandered from father to son, but now we go back to father. Dad was a staunchly religious man. Mass without fail even if it took a team of horses and a sleigh to get there on snow-bound Sundays. On really bad days, he might go alone on his saddlehorse. I have an especially fond memory of going to midnight Christmas Mass one year by sleigh, horse hide robes and a large rock warmed in the oven to keep feet warm. There was a full moon and a clear night to make indelible the beauty of the experience.

Sunday was the Lord's Day. We never once worked in the fields on a Sunday. When hay is cut it needs to be raked before it gets too dry. When grain is ripe it needs to be cut before it starts to shell out on the stem, particularly if the wind blows. Sunday remained the Lord's Day no matter what the weather or the condition of the crops. There was another measure of day when Sunday came. During Lent the family said the rosary nightly *on our knees* no matter what the work day had been.

One day about age ten, I was watching my father straighten a heavy piece of wire about six inches long. I have no recall of how he was going to use it. He kept "eyeing the wire" and persisting in its straightness. I was somehow captivated by his efforts. Now, I think he was intentionally being so deliberate, because when he finished he held it up and said:

"If something is worth doing it is worth doing well."

My strong quiet cornerstone taught me something I have always remembered and for the most part have tried to live by. He was truly a man of the land. He could tell the time of day within fifteen minutes by looking at the location of the sun, and that's in winter or summer.

•

A few days ago I went with four other residents and five department heads of Vantage House to volunteer at the Maryland Food Bank. The editor of *Vantage Views* asked me if I would write a short article about the experience. I insert it here.

Volunteering at Maryland Food Bank

Friday afternoon, March 27th, a number of us went by bus to volunteer at the Maryland Food Bank. Joining us were our Executive Director and five administrators of Vantage House Departments.

The food bank is a non-profit hunger relief organization which partners with communities across the state to distribute food to individuals and families in need. More than 100,000 meals are provided each day, 37 million annually. It is estimated that one in eight Marylanders are food insecure. Children, seniors, working poor, and the homeless are served.

Sources include produce from farms, donations from large food retailers and manufacturers, USDA commodities and purchased foods. A donation of one dollar can provide two meals. Ninety-two percent of donations go directly to food provision.

This was the second experience for some of us. And it was a kind of "let's do it again" afternoon. The warehouse is tremendously large with boxes of dry food stacked high and ready to go on the fleet of trucks which deliver to 1,250 network providers throughout the state. We all worked by a moving conveyor belt, some loading food on the belt and others at various stations each picking certain items off the belt and boxing them up. If you missed it the first time, don't worry it will come around again.

The experience fills one with gratitude for being on this end of the process and not on the receiving end. It opens a window to a world we do well to remember. Those who participated must have slept well that night, partly from fatigue (three hours on your feet and active) and partly from a feeling they had given much more than their time.

•

In memory, I often return to the ranch. When I look out the window, in my imagination I see the prairie, then the foothills leading from the ranch up to the Little Belt Range of mountains, often snowcapped until late July. My early life there taught me the importance of deep faith. Nature rules and the earth responds with heat and cold, lightning, wind and rain, snow and hail. On the ranch we had only our hard work, our determination, our patience and our prayers. When a hailstorm beats the wheat kernels off the stems, when the lightning kills five cows in one strike, when the lack of rain reduces the hay fields to dry grass, when a calf dies at birth because it's a breach delivery, when you have to shoot your horse because he broke his leg in a badger hole when you were chasing cattle, then you can be angry at God or your neighbor or your spouse, or you can accept the life you love and pray to the God who holds you and all things in Hands that hold the stars, the rain clouds, the sun and wind. My father served a fellowship with the Master of the World.

To explain about the five cows: in a bad storm cattle usually move in the direction the wind is blowing. Eventually they are likely to come to a wire fence. If they have their heads on or too near the wires, they may be electrocuted by a nearby lightning strike.

Before leaving the ranch, I'll mention another recurring difficulty. Rancher/farmers had to be inventive in those "good old days." When something was broken, if you couldn't fix it yourself you might have to travel twenty miles to find someone who could *possibly* repair it. If you needed a new part, you had to go fifty miles to get it. In a model T Ford on a rutted dirt road, you would do well to make the round trip in four hours. No wonder, old-timers learned "to do" for themselves.

All this reminds me of my father's youngest brother, Uncle Mark. He worked on the ranch occasionally. Mark was not a patient man and perhaps he didn't like work. And he certainly didn't like horses. The horses knew it. We used to tell stories about Mark out in the field plowing. The horses would stop and he couldn't make them go. He would get off the plow, throw his hat on the ground, jump up and down on it and curse a blue streak, words my father would have frowned on our using. "Thou shalt not take the Lord's name in vain." Maybe the horses objected to Mark's profanity.

•

My early years taught me the sacredness of life. It seemed so clear that crops grew, cows calved and we lived dependent on the largesse of nature, as winter snows, summer rains, sunshine, winds and hail seemed to determine our tomorrows. We were but caretakers in God's world and clearly dependent on God's benefice. Faith was a necessary ingredient in a life so uncertain. The extract of those years remains firmly fixed in my mind and my soul. The imprint of God's presence indelibly marked my life in the persons of my father and mother who cared for me, in the mountains and prairies which enclosed me, in the livestock and wheat fields which provided for me. Nothing has ever shaken the firmness of my beliefs.

•

Many paths and many years since that early life, I was talking with a team of professionals at Taylor Manor Hospital during the lunch hour we occasionally shared. We discussed various topics. One day the mention of God came up and someone asked me if I believed in God.

My response: "I cannot *not* believe in God." I could possibly abandon my religion, I could possibly abandon my spirituality, but I could not abandon my faith. My intellect, my heart, my senses, my being could not accept the concept of a world in which there is no God. To clarify: my faith is monotheism, my religion is Roman Catholic, and my spirituality is my relationship with God, the Author of Life.

•

I find myself feeling lonely and a bit morose lately and wondering why. It might be the weather, since frolicking spring is having a difficult time joining hands with us earthlings. A couple of nice days, then rain or a cold wind from the north. But I also wonder if all this reminiscing may be at the core of my mood change. Reminiscing is not of itself depressing. Most of my memories are of wonderful times shared with Jane either in the doing or in the recounting. The patients I talk about, she knew about because I typically talked to her about my patients. They were people unknown to her; and she served as a sounding board, almost a mentor, for my work. Unpleasant events no longer disturb me in their recall. Military service, the

Reno Easter letter, the night in jail, the conflicted marriage no longer strike an emotional chord.

    The missing ingredient in my current writing is the opportunity to share it with Jane. Since her death, she is "the absence" in everything I do, everything I think. In my mind, Jane was in every scene I now recall and write about, those we lived together and those that occurred before I ever knew her. We often visited the Montana ranch and she knew the buildings and fields and mountains. We walked the road I walked for two years to the one room school house. We visited her Philadelphia together, and walked the streets of the Kensington-Allegheny (K&A) area of her childhood. There were no mysteries between us. Through our reminiscing and lengthy conversations it seems like we relived our childhood and early adulthood together. Jane knew my deceased relatives and I knew hers, not their faces but their stories. We visited the graves of her parents and mine.

•

In December 2005, I discontinued the private practice I had in Ellicott City. At the time, I told Jane I was tired of psychiatry and thought it was time to close shop. She was concerned I was retiring because of her illness and objected to my doing so. But her need was obvious to me and perhaps secretly to her. After Jane died in February 2012, I struggled to hold my life on course and do what I could and should do to "be fine", as I promised Jane I would be.

    For a time, I considered returning to office practice. I would need to reinstate my license and malpractice insurance. There was office space in the same building where I rented before. Then one day the decision became crystal clear to me. I could not go back into practice without Jane present and available to hear about and discuss patients I would be seeing. I could not do it alone.

    I feel so alone as I walk the roads, rummage through the past, uncover bits and pieces, tell the tales and savor the memories. Perhaps that's why I wrote this poem a few months ago. It was published in *Vantage Views*.

BEYOND

Your love of nature
Expanded me
Your love of life
Enriched me

Your love of God
Enlightened me
Your love of me
Stretched my world
Beyond the emptiness
Of life without you

Chapter Seven:
The Dedicated

The months of May and June commemorate people in our lives who in some way provided care for us. Mothers are honored in May, fathers in June, and veterans on Memorial Day. It seems appropriate to give thought and honor to other people who now have that role in our lives.

Residents of Vantage House are surrounded by caregivers day after day, week after week. Often when one compliments or expresses gratitude to a staff member, the response is:

"But we are family." What a loving expression of their view! "We are family!"

Families typically have disparate members, and certainly all of us compose a rather hodgepodge group. But these caregivers in our family manage not just to "put up with us", but to show us kindness to the point of tenderness, responses that go far beyond our spoken need, thoughtful awareness of our limitations, and a keen sense of the pain and sadness we often try to hide from others.

These women and men of Vantage House Staff bring more than just services to this house. They bring consolation to calm our distress, gentleness to soothe our discomfort, patience to restore our strength, and faith in us to help us continue to have faith in ourselves. They often reach out to us before we know to ask for help. And when we do ask for help they respond with a grace and generosity that preserves our sense of dignity and leaves intact our faltering pride.

These "employees" are not just employees! They are more than "caregivers!" They are friends! They are not here just for a salary. They could find the same kind of work with persons who are more independently mobile, persons who can hear what is said the first time it is said, persons who recognize them because they can see them, persons who are always in a pleasant mood because they have no pains, no handicaps, no daily fear of what tomorrow will bring. They **choose** to work with us.

This is a good time to step back a bit from our personal and private anxieties and consider the significance these "friends," these "family members" have in our lives. When I pause to do that, names come flooding into my mind: Travis, Lisa, Karen, Amy, Harold, Chris, Vivian, Musa, Katie, Beulah, Dontre, Ken, Mike, Meriann, Korpo, Marvin, Shirley, Gloria, and the list goes on and on through another fifteen or twenty names. These names have become more important to me than the names of past co-workers, long ago college friends, recent neighbors, and most family members. These are our present, and they have become more important than most people are from out our past.

We are important to them. We are why they are here. However, we must realize those who work here have their own lives, their own cares, and their own feelings. We do not participate directly in their lives, as they do in ours. But we are in their feelings and in their thoughts, and undoubtedly some of us go home with them at times. We may go home with them because they were touched that day by some exchange we had. We may go home with them one day because they feel uneasy for being unable to comfort and console one of us as they wished they could. We may go home with them a day when they feel satisfied because they were able to make someone here a bit happier, a bit more responsive, a bit more peaceful. And there are times when many go home sad because someone who was here is no longer here. The most difficult task for a caregiver is to face the loss of one to whom they gave care. Our caregivers face that loss over and over again at Vantage House, and they are unable to share their grief with us, as we share our grief with them.

Our caregivers leave behind their worries, their troubles, their bad times and their good times and meet us daily with their gentle, thoughtful presence. They listen to our concerns, our complaints, and our conflicts. They accept us on our good days, and our bad days, and our terrible days; and their being with us somehow lifts our spirits and makes the pain a little less, and makes the loneliness not as frightening.

We should think about them often, be grateful for their presence, and honor them for all they do to make our world not just a more livable place but a better place to live.

\+ + + + + + + + + +

The article above was probably written two or three years before Jane's death. At the time, I felt a need to express throughout the Vantage House community the deep gratitude I felt for the kindnesses extended by our staff. Without exception, they showed sincere regard and affection for Jane and always took time to stop and say a few kind words and often embrace her. They extended themselves to put her at ease and make her feel secure and loved. I continue to be grateful for their generous care.

•

I wrote about learning by doing. It began on the ranch. I extended it to my work on houses and apartments doing electrical and plumbing work, carpentry, painting, tiling and whatever the situation demanded. It also served as my template for the administration years in Nevada.

I believe it is accurate to say that is the same way I learned to be a psychiatrist. On the one hand, I still think good psychiatrists are born and not made, although I would have difficulty defending that statement if it were challenged. The experiences of childhood are a significant element for those who become caregivers for others, whatever specific role the caregiver may have. Suffice it to say, I believe good caregivers need to have deep feelings (a good emotional quotient), to be aware of their own feelings and able to recognize them in others.

For the moment, let's consider the training of a good psychiatrist. The four years of medical school, with anatomy, physiology, and all the subspecialty courses provided little that was directly useful in psychiatry as I knew the field. I should also note that psychiatry as I knew it is rapidly changing. We'll review some of the changes later. My experience, which is now about sixty years ago, was *learn by doing*.

My three year residency program was at Seton Psychiatric Institute in Baltimore. During the residency years, we were assigned patients with whom we worked (i.e. talked about their problems, their lives) and then discussed with supervisors who were there to guide and nurture us, point out our weaknesses, correct our errors. The basic learning was in the doing, with supervisors providing some coaching from the sidelines so to speak.

My residency was done at a time when the first psychiatric medicines were just being introduced into the profession. Emphasis at the time was strongly on the "talking part" of psychiatric care. Current psychiatric practice seems to emphasize the use of medication. Let me review a couple of my learning episodes.

•

I was seeing a young man (Max), age eighteen, who had been referred by a physician in Texas. Max was referred because he had forced a cab driver into the trunk of his cab, and then Max tried to drive the cab into Mexico. He was stopped at the border and officers discovered the cab driver locked in the trunk. The young man was charged with kidnapping. He was sent to Seton for psychiatric treatment and, of course, to avoid prosecution in Texas. (He did not have a mental illness requiring hospitalization). Needless to say, the family was quite wealthy and psychiatric hospitalization was acceptable to the court as an alternative. Insurance was rarely an issue for most of the patients at Seton. Hospital stays were often lengthy.

Max was my patient and scheduled to see me 50 minutes once or twice each week. He sparingly gave me some of the details regarding the reason for admission, but he was not forthcoming with information about his family or his past. Beyond being a reluctant patient, he had a hostile attitude, which was clearly deliberate and I found irritating.

One day I was having lunch with one of the highly respected visiting psychiatrists, Dr. Ivan Junk. "Visiting psychiatrists" were from the Baltimore area and admitted their patients to Seton and then participated in their care. I was telling Ivan about Max.

Ivan asked, "What do you really feel about Max?"

I said, "He's a pain in the ass."

To which Ivan responded, "Why don't you tell him that?"

Well, this was far afield from any psychiatric techniques or teaching I ever heard.

The next time Max came to my office it wasn't long before I had the opportunity to pass on Ivan's suggestion.

Max's response: "You're a pain in the ass too."

After that little exchange of feeling and honesty, we got along quite well. I would spend the 50 minute periods looking at charts, cutting my fingernails, or cleaning up my desk. Max might bring something to read, just observe, or pick up one of my books to examine. In between our various activities, we would talk a bit about how he was doing, some of his plans, and a few things about his earlier life. Max left Seton with a healthy attitude about life and kept in touch with me for several years.

•

This is not really a separate topic, but it is a separate patient. After completing residency, I started a private practice in Takoma Park, Md. One of my patients was a fourteen year old girl who was failing in school in spite of her superior intelligence.

After several introductory sessions, one day I said to her, "Mary, can you explain something to me? You know, and I know, and your teachers and parents know that you are a very intelligent girl. Can you explain to me why you are failing in school?"

She thought for a few moments and then replied, "It's quiet anger." She was the middle child of three and felt strongly that her mother did not love her the way she loved the other two. This was her secret way of avenging her mother's behavior toward her. Damaging oneself covertly to hurt someone else is not unusual behavior in us humans.

I always met with the parent or parents of teenagers who were coming for therapy. At that first meeting, I informed them any communication with or from the parents would not be privileged but would be shared with the patient. Any communication from the patient was privileged, not to be communicated to anyone. I asked Mary if she would allow me to have a meeting with her mother without my revealing the content to Mary and if I could speak to her mother about our conversations. She agreed.

I arranged a meeting with her mother and told her about my exchange with Mary. Her mother thought for a while before responding. Then she revealed the problem. When she was pregnant with Mary she discovered her husband was having an affair. She calmly admitted she always felt differently toward Mary because of it. She was obviously relieved to acknowledge the secret that intruded into their relationship. It also opened up a healthier interaction between her and Mary. In a couple of months, Mary was performing well in school and treatment was concluded. And I had learned something valuable about the strength of "quiet anger." Of course, psychiatrists talk about emotions and sublimation and transference and all the other terms of the profession. We learn what the words mean but we only *know what they mean* when we've met them first hand. We learn by doing.

•

Marguerite and I left the ranch in 1947 and went to D.C. where I began the graduate program in Psychology. The indecisive period of my life still dominated. I didn't give the decision a great deal of thought or discussion. It occurred because a priest I knew in Great Falls made the suggestion. At the time, I had little understanding of what psychologists do.

At Catholic University I had two faculty members who had written a popular book in the field: *Catholicism and Psychiatry* by Robert Odenwald, M.D. and James Vander Veldt, O.F.M. I had a class with Doctor Odenwald, who was a prominent Catholic psychiatrist in the area. He asked me to do some writing for him and before long I was writing articles which were published under his name, mostly in Catholic magazines. The articles typically covered relationships between psychiatry and religion. I also did some tutoring for one of his children. It was Bob Odenwald who encouraged me strongly to go to medical school when I finished the doctorate in Psychology. Marguerite and I were good friends with Bob and his wife for many years. The writing and tutoring were a source of some income during medical school years. The writing I did for Bob was profitable not only in his payment, but in opening up the writing field for me.

My decision to go to medical school was a thoughtful and prayerful decision made over a period of time. I went to medical school to become a psychiatrist. I had little attraction to the rest of the medical specialties. At last, I was taking charge of my life in a sound and reasonable manner. I had found my life's goal.

•

I learned something new about psychiatry and about life from every patient I ever saw. There is a particular area of psychiatry in which I still have some learning to do, namely, the subject of sexual identity and all the currently related nuances. I was a psychiatric resident from 1957 to 1960. At that time, the general attitude of psychiatrists was that homosexuality was a curable illness. It was listed in the Diagnostic and Statistical Manual (DSM) as a psychiatric disorder.

I am almost embarrassed to say that, with many others, I attempted to treat these individuals with the goal of changing this "sick" and, yes I must add, "sinful" behavior, or so I thought at that time. In my defense, I will add the diagnosis was not removed from the DSM until 1973, and then by the vote of a majority of psychiatrists with a fair percentage of dissenters. Over subsequent years, my thinking on the subject has markedly changed due to educational opportunities and occasions to know personally and to have as patients, persons of various sexual orientations and identities.

The topic is an extensive one and I do not feel competent to discuss it with any mastery. Suffice it to say I make no mental, emotional or moral judgments about those with sexual identities or orientations included in GLBTQA groupings. I have treated some of them for the emotional conflicts and life problems usual in psychiatric patients. To obtain further information on Gay, Lesbian, Bisexual, Transgender, Questioning (Queer) and Asexual (Ally) persons, you might consult the internet. In my opinion, it is important to avoid making judgments about persons based on any of these "identities."

The current DSM lists a diagnosis of Gender Dysphoria designating individuals who experience distress and inner conflict because their experienced/expressed gender does not correspond with their assigned/natal gender. To complete the listing, I will add intersex individuals who have both male and female genitalia. Finally, cuigender or cissexual individuals experience the gender of their genitalia.

•

During my residency, I missed an opportunity to appreciate a potential lesson about the subject of sexual identity. A priest from a Benedictine Community was admitted to Seton. I was assigned as his psychiatrist. He had just completed graduate studies in Europe. On return to his community, he informed his superiors he was homosexual. He was sent for treatment to cure this "perversion."

He readily informed me he had no desire to change and he intended to leave the hospital to return to his community. I am shocked to realize what I'm going to tell you could occur in the early 60's. At that time under Maryland law, a person could be held in a psychiatric hospital against their will based on an evaluation and signed affidavits by two psychiatrists not employed by the hospital. After a brief period of time, I believe the patient could request a court hearing and go before a judge for final decision as to the need for involuntary hospitalization. I requested the two evaluations and they were done by two private psychiatrists from Baltimore.

Every weekday morning all the residents met with the Hospital Director, Dr. Leo Bartemeir, and the Hospital Clinical Director, Dr. Lou Cleary, a number of the nursing staff, the social work staff and the hospital psychologists. We met in a large room with a long table for the twelve or more resident staff and the two chiefs. There were chairs around the sides of the room for psychologists, social workers, and nursing staff. It was a very impressive setting. Residents were expected to report on their newly assigned cases.

I reported on the new priest-patient indicating his diagnosis as well as his determination to leave the hospital. I also reported with a sense of pride, I had obtained the two affidavits preventing his departure.

Doctor Cleary quietly said, "Now that you have him, what are you going to do with him?"

I'm grateful he didn't expect an answer. I would have made an even bigger fool of myself. It was a learning experience I will never forget.

I truly believe the question would never have entered Dr. Bartemeir's thinking. He was a well-known bigwig of the psychoanalytic world. He believed cure could occur with psychoanalysis.

Doctor Cleary was so right, but it took me another four or five years before I learned from life experiences and from friends and patients that these "diversities" are not illnesses and never were illnesses. Just as we do not chose our sex, neither do we chose our sexual identity.

About a week after the staff meeting I mentioned, I discharged the priest to go home to his community where he would likely have been laicized or ostracized or both. I hope the first. I let him go without the professional grace to apologize. Of course, I'm assuming I clung to the adage familiar from the ranch: "you can lead a horse to water—" No doubt that's how I justified my behavior at the time and went merrily along planning to "cure" homosexuals.

•

Recently, I noted several states have passed laws forbidding the use of "conversion" or "reparative" therapy, terms used by practitioners who still claim to reverse same sex attraction in individuals. In the late 90's when I was a staff psychiatrist at Taylor Manor Hospital in Ellicott, Md., a newly hired psychiatrist was terminated because of his determination to use conversion therapy on the adolescent unit. In the past month, President Obama commented that conversion therapy should be against the law in all the states, a position supported by the American Psychiatric Association. The President's comment resulted from the suicide of a child after the failure of conversion therapy. The nation has come a long way in the last sixty years to eliminate prejudice regarding the lifestyle of those who by nature belong to one of the GLBTQA groups. But there is still a long way to go.

It is worth mentioning the people of Ireland have recently passed a law defining marriage as the union of two persons irrespective of their sexual identity. Ireland is a predominantly Catholic country. Perhaps the Catholic Church will someday follow their lead.

•

Reverend John Harvey, O.S.F.S. founded "Courage," a spiritual support group for gays and lesbians which advocates sexual abstinence. Cardinal Terence Cooke of New York conceived the idea and enlisted Father Harvey to carry it forward. Father Harvey taught medical and spiritual ethics at DeSales University in Center Valley, Pa. He also taught at St. Joseph Seminary in New York and Seton Hall University in New Jersey. He was awarded the Cardinal Cooke Medal of Peace on October 6, 2003. I believe he was considered a rather conservative theologian at that time.

Courage International remains an approved apostolate of the Roman Catholic Church to minister to those with same-sex attractions. It currently includes 110 chapters worldwide. Goals of the organization are to promote chastity, piety, and the support of compassionate and charitable works.

•

I bring up Father Harvey at this time partly because of his work in the area of sexual diversity. The subject does bring him to mind. In addition, Father John was an extremely important person in my life and one to whom I am forever greatly indebted.

When first I was in love with Jane, my strong Catholic background prodded my conscience severely. I found it difficult to allow myself to even think about divorce. I felt a strong need for spiritual guidance. As a graduate student at Catholic University, I taught a number of undergrad seminarians. I kept in touch with two or three who belonged to the Oblates of St. Francis de Sales, Father Harvey's order. I called one of them and asked whom he would recommend as a spiritual director.

Father Harvey was a godsend to me. He was kind, insightful, patient, and he made himself available to my need. I saw him on a fairly regular basis for at least two years. Eventually, he supported me in the decision to get a divorce. It was a grace right from heaven, as far as I was concerned. He met Jane on one occasion when I brought her to the religious house where he lived.

The night the police came to take me to the Montgomery County jail I asked if I could make one phone call before I left the house. I called Jane and told her what was happening. She called Father Harvey who was at that time in Philadelphia. He took the first train available to Washington. Jane met him at the station and took him to his residence. He came to see me the following morning at the jail.

We stayed in touch through the years. He visited us in Reno and stayed with us a couple of days. When we lived in Baltimore many years later, one night we were awakened by a phone call about 11 pm. Father John was at the Baltimore depot and someone from his community had failed to come for him. He asked if I could pick him up. Of course, I got him and brought him to the house. He and I sat and talked a couple of hours over a drink. Jane had a bed ready for him when he was ready for bed. He was a blessing to us both!

Chapter Eight:
T'ain't Funny

No one needs tell us the world has changed. We have witnessed remarkable changes from the days of the Dick Tracey wrist watch to the complexity of the digital age and how it affects the world of our children and grandchildren. Some changes have been more subtle and difficult to adopt.

Changes in "politically correct" and "socially correct" language and subjects have undergone radical alterations. When we were younger we heard or told jokes, made critical comments, or related negative stories about persons of different color, different ethnic groups, different beliefs, or different sexual orientation. Words we formerly said quite readily and heard without offense are now, not just bad taste, but considered abusive to those they refer to and appropriately offensive to those who hear them used.

In the not too distant past, we described people with various handicaps using descriptive words that did not strike us as offensive. Much of that terminology is no longer considered suitable. When I was in medical school in the 50's we regularly spoke about retarded people, insane people, the crippled, the deaf, and the blind. Those terms are no longer acceptable in referring to these impairments. We now refer to the mentally challenged, the mentally ill, the physically handicapped, the hearing impaired, and the visually impaired.

A medical term many of us have probably never heard or used is "mild cognitive impairment" (MCI). This term refers to the memory loss many older individuals experience and may include remote memory loss and/or short term memory loss. "Mild cognitive impairment" occurs in 10 to 20% of persons age 65 and older. Of those with mild cognitive impairment, 10 to 20% will progress to "dementia" in their 80's. Statistics indicate that by age 85 one in every three people will have some form of cognitive impairment.

"Dementia" is one of the ugliest and most inappropriate terms in medical use. One does not have to be a Latin scholar to know the word means "out of your mind." Dementia patients are not "out of their minds." They are very much in their minds, and it is a dark and lonely and frightening place.

In our present general culture and in the regular and rather close contact we have with one another in Vantage House, it seems appropriate and almost necessary for each of us to recognize the importance of using terms (at least in a group setting) that are not offensive to those who experience impairment. We make jokes with our friends about being "half blind" or "so deaf I can't hear myself think." And it is not unusual to hear a few friends engaging in one-up-man's ship about memory loss. However, in reality none of these conditions is in any way a laughing matter when significant impairment is involved.

To be appropriate, we should speak of others as visually impaired, hearing impaired, movement impaired, and memory or cognitively impaired. But we should not be critical of other residents who may still speak of someone having "poor hearing," "poor eyesight," or "poor memory." It is important for all of us to be sensitive and to respect the impairment of others and give some serious thought to how their life has changed as a result. For them, it is not amusing but a disturbing and grave matter. Those of us who are more fortunate might remember, "But for the grace of God. . ."

+ + + + + + + + + +

I have superficially referred to my children, but not at all, to Jane's. The children were a tremendous loss for both of us and resulted in troubled relationships for many years and in many ways. There is no doubt each of them suffered in her or his own way as a result of our decision to leave Maryland and move to Reno. One may rightfully accuse Jane and me of selfishness in what we did. Yes, we were focused on *our needs, our desires, our lives*. We did what we thought was right *for us*. At the time, we were both profoundly aware of the damage our marriages were causing those living in each household. In the overall scheme of things, we came to believe what we did also turned out better for the children.

Marguerite and I had five children, two girls and three boys. In 1966, my oldest daughter was nineteen and my youngest daughter was six. The summer of that year, my three sons were in Montana at the ranch with my brother and his wife. On my trip to Reno to apply for the job, I returned home via Montana and told the boys about my plans. (Their relationship with their mother was one of the reasons I made arrangements for them to be in Montana). I told them I planned to have them with Jane and me in Nevada after necessary court proceedings. I did not properly foresee the future. I did not know I would *"sell"* them in exchange for my own freedom.

Jane and her first husband, Tom, had three children, a boy of fourteen and two girls, ages seven and five (as of 1966). After her divorce in Virginia, Jane went to court in Maryland for custody of her children. By then, Tom had been remarried for some time. Jane had indeed "abandoned" her children in moving to Richmond. Her physical fear of Tom was of no consequence in court. It is said that, "Fate plays funny tricks." The judge who heard the case was in court for the first day after some sort of brain surgery. In addition, the judge's wife had just separated from him, and his young son was sitting in court waiting for his father.

The judge gave custody of the two girls to Tom. Then he took Jane's son and his own son into chambers where he asked Jane's son which parent he wanted to be with. Philip was totally opposed to going with his father. His custody was given to Jane. At the time, we left Philip with his maternal grandmother in Philadelphia, anticipating he would come to Reno when we got settled there. Jane's mother had always been close to Jane's children.

Jane was allowed to see her two girls briefly before we left for Reno. My sons had not returned from Montana. My older daughter was away. I saw no one before leaving. The loss was heartache for us both. Jane cried every night for months. It remained a delicate topic for her for many years. She always felt there was an unspoken condemnation by people who knew the court awarded the children to Tom. I believe no one ever said anything to her, but the feeling was there. "In a divorce the mother always gets the children." It is one of those judgments many people make in total ignorance of any facts relating to a particular situation.

Jane wrote to the girls but, we later discovered, Tom never gave them the letters. He refused to let the girls visit, even after his son was living with us in Reno. After we were in Reno two years, Tom called the house one day. He was in Reno with the girls. He would bring them to see their mother if I was not in the house. He came with the girls, but would not let Jane touch either of them. After this cruel visit, we hired an attorney in Maryland and took Tom to court. He was ordered to let the girls visit, which they did several times over the ensuing years.

I experienced a variety of conflicts with all five of my children, conflicts scattered over many years. I essentially had no contact with my youngest daughter, Patricia, until this past year. My daughters were always reserved in their relationship with Jane. I was out of contact with Paul, from the time he was twelve until he was thirty-two. We were alienated by an episode which occurred in Reno involving strong emotional reactions to an unfortunate event. He and his younger sister, Patricia, were with us at the time. Paul was a lovable twelve year-old and had a warm relationship with Jane. There was some minor incident between Jane and Patricia. Paul had a feeling of being his sister's protector. He wrote a letter to his mother and in the letter called Jane a "witch." Unfortunately, Jane saw the open letter in his room and read it. She was deeply offended and wanted me to send the two children home. Jane came first for me throughout our life together. We sent the two children home as soon as arrangements could be made.

Yes, it was another of life's mistakes; no, my mistakes. The matter could have been worked out with a little time. Jane was not an unforgiving person. But at least it was one of those mistakes that somehow turned out wonderfully in the end. I believe the relationship Jane and I finally developed with Paul was richer and deeper than it ever might otherwise have been. The three of us seemed to savor our belated relationship with increasing pleasure over the last years.

In 1992 when we lived in Maine, Paul's current wife encouraged him to visit us. The wounds were quickly healed. I see them often now and we are close. He became very fond of Jane and during her illness he visited regularly in spite of his own busy schedule as a dentist. He and my oldest son, Bob, both became attached to Jane and both of them called her, "Mom." It pleased her and me as well.

Jane and I have one child who lives in Demarest, N.J. She has two girls, now ages seventeen and fifteen. Thankfully, Laura was divorced about ten years ago. Two of my sons, Jane's son, and one of Jane's daughters are also divorced.

Looking back from my present perspective, I am grateful Jane and I went to Reno even though it meant separation from the children. I have seen too much of the bitterness and bickering and bargaining that go on when children share time with separated parents. It can work out well in some cases, but Marguerite and I would never have agreed on what we wanted for or expected from our children. We had few common values and no common dreams. Similarly, Jane and Tom were at opposite poles in terms of parental expectations and life goals. Proximity would not have permitted harmonious living for any of us.

•

Some religions take a strict position about divorce, basically forbidding it. Certainly divorce should not be entered into lightly, nor should marriage. But, we all make mistakes and some marriages are clearly mistakes. In my opinion, there is a need for divorce when children are subjected to an enduringly hostile, bitter, and unloving relationship between their parents. Whether or not there is physical abuse in the home, such a relationship establishes emotional abuse and produces an environment that is harmful to the children and deprives them of the parental connections, which are important during their maturation years. In my experience, emotional abuse is more damaging than physical abuse. It is typically not visible to others and frequently goes unrecognized by the victim. My years of psychiatric work with emotionally ill teenagers and adults have consistently reinforced this opinion.

•

I mentioned James Van der Veldt, O.F.M. who was a professor of mine at Catholic University. When I was a psychiatric resident, James's brother Albert was a fellow resident. Al was also a Franciscan priest, who had returned from missionary work because he had contracted malaria. Al and I became good friends and worked together at Seton on a study, which was published in the March 1961 edition of the *American Journal of Nervous and Mental Diseases* titled: *Psychiatric Illness in Hospitalized Catholic Religious*. We later did a paper on the same subject but in relation to alcoholism, published in the 1962 edition of the *Quarterly Journal for the Study of Alcoholism*. These may have been the first published psychiatric studies about Catholic religious.

After we finished our residency, Al became the Director of the Child Guidance Clinic at the Catholic University of America. I opened a psychiatric practice in Takoma Park, MD and was consulting at the Child Guidance Clinic and teaching at C.U.A. Al and I continued our friendship and saw each other regularly. I never discussed my marital situation with Al and sometimes wonder why I didn't. He was certainly my best friend and we tended to confide in each other. He and his brother James both knew Marguerite and we often had dinner together.

Fortunately, Al one day confided in me he sometimes had chest pain but had not recently been to a physician. One rainy Saturday evening, probably in 1962, Father James called me with the news Al died that afternoon while sitting in a movie theater in Baltimore. His body was in a Baltimore hospital awaiting determination of cause of death. James asked me to go and to sign the death certificate. He desperately pleaded with me to do so, saying he could not tolerate the thought of an autopsy being performed. Marguerite and I drove from Bethesda to Baltimore. I saw the body and signed the death certificate putting down as cause "cardiac failure" or some similar phrase. I did it based on the comment Al had made to me a month or so before the event. Was it ethical? I really don't know. Was it the right thing to do? It was what I did.

•

I will say something about my current exercise schedule, since health at my age is a treasured asset. At the time of this writing and for the past two years or more, I have followed a rather fixed routine. I get up at 5:30 a.m. and go to the in-house exercise room. I exercise for an hour: fifteen minutes on the elliptical for one and a half miles, seventeen minutes on the treadmill for one mile, and fifteen minutes on the bicycle for three and a half miles. That nets over 350 calories. Then I exercise on three upper-body weight machines to finish the hour. Monday through Friday I attend one hour to one and a half hours of exercise classes. Every afternoon, weather permitting, I walk around Lake Kittamaqundi which is a three mile walk. Why do I do all this? Certainly not so I can boast about it. It wouldn't be worth it. I do it because I can, because God has given me the physical health that enables it, because I treasure the gift. It enriches the body, mind and spirit which I pray to maintain until God calls me home. It also fills my day with value. I feel the need to keep active, busy.

There is an additional value in the morning exercises and in the afternoon walks. I mentioned the routine of prayers I say during the morning exercises. They follow a pattern and cover my lifetime: the people I knew, the places I lived, the major events that occurred. The afternoon walks are often times to say the rosary and to just find God in the sky, the water, robins, and geese and squirrels, the trees that surround me. It is often a time I remember blessings, especially the blessing Jane was in my life. It's the walk we often took when she was well enough to go. A walk filled with her child-like fascination with God's world and how her perception of it always brought me something new to see and to appreciate.

The walk to the lake became a life ritual after we moved to Vantage House. For years, we walked on sidewalks where we lived, but this freedom from traffic and the privacy of the woods were especially attractive. I prefer to walk alone now. In addition to prayer and some meditative time, it is a good time for just thinking.

Prior walks with Jane inspired this recent poem.

MEMORIES
I sat
On a bench at the lake
The sun
Said "let me warm you"
I found
The comfort of her rays.

I watched
The last leaves falling
Branches
Kissed them on their way
Earth held them
In the embrace of autumn.

I felt
The leaves of memory
Slip away
Into dying cells of mind
She's gone
This is another day.

I'm cold
Dark has filtered in
The sun

Was gone before I knew
The sky
No longer holds me.

•

Today was a beautiful afternoon, a late spring day in May. I took the usual walk. The trees have responded to abundant spring rain and have closed out the view of neighboring buildings and the nearby street with its six lanes of cars. I was surrounded by the unending green of the trees and bushes and patches of infinite blue sky showing above me. I felt like God was embracing me. I was not alone. And I wrote the following poem.

MISSING
The trees sing out you name
In a plaintive sort of tune
They ask me where you are
And will they see you soon

The birds join in the song
And the chorus fills the air
I say you've gone away
But I see you everywhere

Since I'm back to writing about walks to the lake I will include a piece I wrote sometime in the last year. I had just returned from a walk and run and was feeling exhilarated. I needed to write about it for my own satisfaction.

Confessions of an Avid Runner

This is a personal story, but I'll take the risk. I hadn't run in years—twenty, maybe thirty or more. So long ago I can't remember. No reason to run, walking got me where I wanted to go. Jane and I walked hand in hand for almost fifty years. Why would I want to run? In later years, her Alzheimer's pace was tediously slow, annoyingly so I must confess.

Once when I chided her about it, she responded, "You should be grateful I'm here and can walk at all."

So right! So right!

After Jane was gone and I walked alone, I began to fantasize about running, wondering what it would be like, wondering if I could. It seems like such a simple thing. Then one day last fall, I decided to try it. What a thrill! What satisfaction! What a gift! All of those. Over a few weeks I pushed the distance to ¼ mile. But I wanted more. Now I run intermittently during my usual three mile walk. I have no doubt I run at least ¼ of the three mile distance. And I keep pushing it a little more.

Why do I run? Why do birds fly? Why do cats climb trees? Because they can. I run because I can, and as I do my heart is full of gratitude to the One who gives me the body, the strength, and the will. I run for the satisfaction and the joy it brings.

Running takes me back to the "wonder" times of youth, riding my horse at dawn to bring the work horses in from the pasture, the satisfaction of pitching hay to feed hungry cattle on the ranch, the pleasure of wrapping my mind around philosophy in college, and the sense of accomplishment in completing work on a degree. Running connects me with the world of nature, the starkness of winter, the dawning of spring, the lush of summer, and the painted autumns.

Why doesn't walking do the same? Running my heart beats faster, stronger and the world rushes in and fills me with its message of life, of beauty, of something beyond my pace, beyond my reach. And deep inside I know whether I run or walk I'm on my way home.

•

A few pages back I mentioned the term "emotional quotient". That's a term I use to describe the "feeling capacity", the breadth and depth of the emotional responsiveness of individuals. I'm not aware if others use the term. Most people are familiar with "intelligence quotient" and recognize its common usage to describe the intellectual capacity and abilities of someone. Intelligence quotient (IQ) is considered to be a product of both heredity and environment, the latter term referring primarily to the early experiences of the person.

I strongly believe the emotional quotient (EQ) of people markedly varies and depends on the same factors of heredity and environment, weighing heavily on the factor of environment. Genetic factors are undoubtedly involved but early relationships with caregivers and those influential in the child's environment provide important influence and role models during critical years. The extent of a person's ability to react emotionally to others plays an important role in particular life relationships and in certain life tasks.

Bluntly put, EQ varies from warm and cuddly to "stick of wood" level. These are the ends of the spectrum with everyone falling somewhere in between. I believe emotional warmth and responsiveness are qualities essential to both parties in a close and loving relationship. I believe these qualities are extremely important for parents in the rearing of their children. When I treated adolescents, after a time I began to feel I knew what the EQ of their parents was. I would ask the patient to describe family exchanges at meal time, bed time, vacation time, party time, and talk time. And the parents and their role in the child's life became real, and that expanded my understanding of the adolescent's behaviors.

A friend gave me a bookmark the other day. It said, "The way we talk to our children becomes their inner voice" (Peggy O'Mara). How well said!

I have known, I have treated, and I have associated with people who seemed truly incapable of deep personal feelings. They could express sympathy, or even anger, for the impoverished in a foreign country, for the plight of persons displaced by wars, for the harm to others by discrimination. But for them these "feelings" were really expressions of opinions about remote situations and distant individuals. They came from the mind, not from the heart. They *know* these situations are abusive or outright wrong, but they do not have an appreciation of how the victims *feel*.

In treating people who are married or in a significant relationship, I have frequently found this "stick of wood syndrome" as the basic problem. The patient is struggling to understand and accommodate to the partner's lack of emotional competence. Marriage counseling is often recommended for these couples. With that help, they may come to understand the emotional limitations that are an integral part of their relationship and learn to accept them. They have to leave behind expectations of a significant change in EQ. They must come to understand there are persons who do not have the capacity for emotional intimacy even though they may do well as intellectual and/or sexual partners.

People with low EQ's do poorly in caregiving roles. As administrators or supervisors they may do a good job but they are probably not well liked by their employees. They have that "ability to inflict pain," but they can't empathize with those who hurt. Politicians capitalize on "intellectualized emotional expressions", though they may lack the depth of feelings required by the words they speak. As a practicing Catholic, I think it is fair to say most members of the Church hierarchy appear to have rather low EQ's. On the other hand, Pope Francis demonstrates an obvious and genuine sensitivity to the needs of others.

People with low EQ's may do quite well in life, especially if they have high IQ's. Persons who are intellectually bright and observant of others learn to imitate the words and mannerisms of those who are genuinely sensitive and emotionally responsive. Their duplicity can win, at least temporarily, the trust and affection of those who are looking for warm and tender feelings in a relationship. It usually takes trusting persons a rather long time before they become aware that all is not as it seems.

Even after discovering the truth of the situation, the duped person often says, "It's so hard to believe that person didn't really have the feelings they seemed to be expressing."

Dealing with a person with a low emotional quotient is like dealing with a five year old. If they want something badly, they will promise you anything to get it and sound as sincere as can be. But five year olds do not have the intelligence required to make a completely deceptive case for themselves. The adult with a good IQ does.

Before leaving the topic of EQ, I will venture a sexist comment and say in my experience, both as an individual and as a psychiatrist, women generally have higher EQ's than males. In a problematic marriage, it was more common for a woman to come for help, often because the husband was trying to convince her she had problems when in fact he was a "stick of wood."

John Bowlby's classic work "Attachment" (Basic Books, Inc. 1969) is still an excellent source for further information about the origin of emotional reactions, how they develop, how they are damaged and how they cause damage.

•

I landed in jail a second time. While we were still in Reno, my oldest son, Bob, moved there with his wife. There were troubled times between them and my son came to stay with us for a few days. One evening, he and I went to get his car which his wife had refused to let him have. He needed it for work. Shortly after we arrived a police car drove up. There was a ruckus, no blows, no foul words, mostly my son's boiling anger and the over solicitous attitude of the police for the wife. The police took Bob and me to the Sparks jail. (Sparks is a suburb of Reno and the location of the hospital). The chief of police had previously, at my request, given a talk at the hospital on substance abuse. He and I were on good terms. I asked the police to call him after we got to the jail. He instructed them to release us if we left one hundred dollars as security. We had little money with us, so the police allowed me to go home to get my check book. When I got home, I explained to Jane what happened.

She replied with a smile, "I hope you're not making a habit of this."

I went to the Nugget Casino, cashed the check and picked up my son. There was a small item in the Reno paper the next day. Charges were dropped. After we went to bed that night, my son left the house, walked to where his car was, hot-wired it, and brought it to the hospital grounds. Later, rumors suggested the policeman and the wife had been "quite friendly for some time" before this encounter.

Chapter Nine:
Trip to Montana

In August, I went to Montana with my son to celebrate my 93rd birthday with twenty-six family members. Although I lived in Montana until I was nineteen, I learned some facts I never knew before.

Great Falls, Montana was the formidable spot where Lewis and Clark spent valuable time portaging around the falls to continue their journey to find the "inland waterway to the Pacific." Just outside Great Falls we visited Giant Springs, one of the largest fresh water springs in the world. The spring pours out 338 million gallons of water each day and the water remains at a constant temperature of fifty-four degrees Fahrenheit year round.

The water originates from the snow pack in the Little Belt Mountains sixty miles away and comes through cracks in the 250 million year old Madison Limestone Formation. The spring runs into the shortest river in the world, the Roe River, which courses 200 feet to empty into the Missouri River.

The Missouri River is the longest river in North America and runs 2,341 miles before it empties into the Mississippi River at St. Louis, MO. The Missouri drainage is from ten States and two Canadian Provinces.

Fort Benton, Montana, on the Missouri was the most inland port in America. The area was explored by Lewis and Clark in 1805. The first steamboat arrived there in 1860. It thrived as a port until the 1880s brought the arrival of the Great Northern Railway, built by James Hill.

My maternal grandfather was a friend of James Hill and in 1888 brought his family to Montana in a boxcar provided by James Hill, who wanted my grandfather to write stories about the frontier so travelers and shippers would use the new railroad. It is interesting that my father, from eastern Canada, worked his way to Montana in 1898 building fences for the Great Northern Railroad.

Four McAllister's immigrated to Montana from Eastern Canada, and I am the eldest of the four children who still survive from their twenty-six offspring. Our ranch was in the foothills of the Little Belt Mountains.

Three days after celebrating my birthday I climbed Square Butte with my two sons, my son-in-law, and my niece. We parked at an elevation of 4,000 feet. We started the climb at 7 a.m. and at 12:15 p.m. we reached the top, an elevation of 5,864 feet. We had to find paths through thick sage brush at the base of the mountain and we zigzagged up the steep sides to find a passable access through the rocks and trees. Much of the climb was steeper than the stairwells in our building. (The Empire State Building is 1200 feet high).

My sons and son-in-law carried the food and water, so I had no backpack. We took apples, tangerines, almonds, dried apricots, granola bars and lots of water. Each of us carried water and drank lightly and frequently. After lunch, we spent over two hours fighting our way through thick young trees to reach three different rocky ledges on the mountain edge, each with a breathtaking view.

Going down in the slide-rock was actually more treacherous than climbing up. Breathing was easier but the danger of falling was much greater. It took over four hours to come down the mountain, make our way back through the sagebrush and reach the car at 7:30 p.m.

I don't mean to brag, but I'm probably the only ninety-three year old person who ever climbed Square Butte. I'm thinking of getting the shoes bronzed.

+ + + + + + + + + +

The above was written in the fall of 2012. I hadn't been to Montana for several years because of Jane's illness. Three of my children had been going for several years to attend the Cowboy Poetry Gathering in Lewistown each August. They were all fans of Cowboy Poetry and had become so partly because of my nephew, Jim McAllister. Jim was a well-known and loved cowboy poet since the eighties. He won several awards and made three CD's of his work.

Jim participated in the Cowboy Poetry Gathering for the last time in 2013. He had a stroke later that year and died after about eighteen months of partial paralysis and aphasia. Although my oldest son Bob and my daughter Fran continue to go, I lost interest in going after the death of Jim. He was Don and Helen's only son and my favorite nephew. I admired him and saw in him many qualities of my father.

In 2012, it was my son Paul who took me back to Montana and the ranch that has always been vividly present in my mind. As mentioned in the article, I had a wonderful birthday with relatives I hadn't seen in thirty to forty years. Paul and I visited the places I mentioned and the mountain climb was something I never dreamed of doing. As a boy, Square Butte was a mountain I saw every day from the ranch. It was about forty miles away as the crow flies. It looked perfectly flat across its lengthy expanse and stood alone in a long range of mountains called the Highwoods. I always wondered what was on the flat top. When I finally got there I found the answer was thick small trees. There had been a forest fire on the top several years before and the forest service simply let it burn. Since forest fires always go up the mountain, there was no place for it to go. Now the top is covered with new-growth trees.

•

Other residents at Vantage House expressed curiosity about cowboy poetry. Eventually, I wrote an article about cowboy poets. It follows:

Cowboy Poets

When I mentioned going to Montana to hear cowboy poets, many people asked me:

"What are cowboy poets?"

I responded rather glibly, "They are a new generation of Native Americans." I know of no lawyer poets, carpenter poets or teacher poets gathering frequently to recite their poetry to one another.

Cowboy poets date back to the late 1880s or earlier. A poetry classic, "Laska," was written by Frank Desprez, a man who came from England and worked as a cowboy for three years. "Laska" was first published in England in 1882. Cowboys inhabited the lands of the Apaches, the Sioux, the Navajo, the Cheyenne, the Assiniboine, and other Indian tribes of the West. The spirit of the cowboy rose from the dust, the ashes, and the ghosts of those first Native Americans. And like them, the cowboy lives with the glorious beauty and harsh realities of nature and identifies with the mountains and valleys, the sky and stars, the wind, and the howl of the wolf and the coyote.

Like artists who need to paint what they see and writers who need to write what they feel, cowboys need to paint with words the world they view and express the feelings that overflow to a page. And like the Indians before them, they gather and tell their stories, now love poems, ballads of the west, and tales from long ago.

Like the Indians, the cowboy's life is disappearing slowly, quietly, and more peacefully than was the fate of the Indians. They are beginning to write poems about the invasion of government, such as introducing wolves into National Parks (wolves leave parks and kill young calves), the "Hollywood and Vine folk" who buy large tracts of land to subdivide for "ranchettes."

The poem, "Men of the Open Range," (by Mike Logan) ends with this sad reflection:

"I can see the ghosts of riders
Movin' out across the dawn
The gold of day's first comin'
Paints their passin'. Now they're gone."

Considering those words, I think Mike Logan would say, "Mama, don't let your babies grow up to be cowboys."

•

There is a beautiful poem my nephew wrote, which I'm going to insert here. I read this poem during three or four programs given by some of the residents at Vantage House. Individuals often asked me for a copy and one resident told me he used it in the eulogy at his wife's funeral. By the way, Jim composed all his poetry in his head when he was out riding to check on his cattle. He never put any of it on paper until later years when his wife encouraged him to write the poems down.

NEVER
Would I write you a love poem
No it's just not in the cards
No I'd never write a love poem
For it would be so hard

To open up my heart
And pour out my very soul
Put my deepest thoughts on paper
For the whole wide world to know

About the way I feel
When you hold me in your arms
No I'll never write a love poem
I'll never talk about your charms

Rather I'll write about the mountains
And the sparkling mountain streams
The wind sighing through the tree tops
Stirring up those longing dreams

Of the softness in your voice
As you whisper in my ear
No I'll never write a love poem
From me you'll never hear

Poems about the prairie
And the cowboy way of life
Poems about the old times
And the hardships and the strife

I'll write about my mother
And I'll write about old Dad
I'll write about good horses
And some others that I've had

But I'd never write a love poem

Robert J. McAllister M.D., Ph.D.

For never would I dare
Take a chance revealing secrets
That you and I alone must share

I'll write about the meadowlark
The coyote and curlew
But I'll never write of love
And I'll never write of you

I'll never tell of times
When we're lying side by side
Instead I'll write of early mornings
When I've saddled up to ride

In search of straying cattle
And the birds are all in song
And I'll think of you so sweet
And how I'll miss you while I'm gone

But I'll not mention your caress
That sends this tingling down my spine
That tingling that reminds me
I am yours and you are mine

Oh I might speak of you
In some offhand sort of way
But I'll never write a love poem
For fear it might betray

That love best left unspoken
To nurture there and grow
Deep down within our hearts
And by now you surely know

Why I'll never write a love poem
No I'm afraid it can't be done
So I'd better stop right now

Before I end up writing one.
(Jim McAllister)

If this kind of poetry interests you, I would suggest you look up "Laska" on the internet. It too is a beautiful though tragic love story.

•

At this time in life, it is interesting to me how strongly I identify with cowboy life—the ranch, the prairies and mountains of Montana. Perhaps these poems give you some idea why. It sometimes feels crowded with the staff and the two hundred plus residents who live in this building. Columbia continues to grow and develop and I feel buried in the buildings and bewildered among all the cars. I miss the broad view of the world with mountains on the horizon. Most of all I miss the stars.

When Jane and I visited Montana in later years, we would go at a time when there was a new moon. Then the stars would be more visible without the competition of a bright moon. Some nights I would get up about two a.m. and go outside to see the stars. There were no interfering lights. The sky was so blanketed with stars it looked like there was hardly space between them. The clear air of Montana contributes to the brilliance of their shine. In the book *Cold Mountain* by Charles Frazier, the woman, waiting for her lover to return, lays on the grass to look at the stars. She has the sensation of "falling upwards." One night, I had that very sensation as I stood looking up. It was so real it was frightening. I was plummeting upward. I was soaring through space. The sensation was so profound, so dizzying I went in the house as if for safety.

•

In the past year, I've had a slightly similar sensation on occasions when I go to Saturday Mass at the Shrine of Saint Anthony. When I first go in and kneel for several minutes with my eyes closed and just an awareness of being there, I have a feeling I am being pulled upward, almost as if I'm floating on a cloud. It continues as I maintain the posture. I don't suggest there is some deep spiritual significance in it, but I do remember one winter day when Jane and I sat on a bench by the grotto there.

On cold, but sunny, Sundays in the winter, Jane and I would sometimes drive to the Shrine after we had lunch at the mall. She was too ill to go to Sunday Mass by this time. She could no longer accommodate to the crowd. On this particular Shrine Sunday, as we were talking about our life and the impact and significance of her illness, she looked at me and said:

"I will meet you here."

Neither of us made any further comment about her remark. It remains fixed in my mind. So, perhaps my imagination plays its part in the sensation of being pulled upwards.

•

We consciously measure life in terms of hours and days using our clocks and calendars. In addition to these measurement methods, we sometimes measure not in terms of time passing, but in relation to the time still left to us—a time of course unknown. But, it is still a question many people have, particularly older people.

Did you ever buy a car and wonder: "Will this be the last car I ever buy?"

Have you bought the last house you'll ever buy? Jane and I thought that six times, each time without verbalizing, "This will be our house for the rest of our life." This tick-tock of living becomes more conscious and even intrusive as we get older. Will this be the last tube of toothpaste I will ever need? How many stamps should I buy this time? Will there be Christmas cards again in my life?

•

I probably have an unusual distinction among all the residents at Vantage House. I have lived in this retirement community longer than I have lived anywhere else in my life. I'm referring to a continuous time of occupancy. I left the ranch at age eight to go to school. I only lived one more year at the ranch when I returned home from the service in 1945. During our twenty years of marriage, Marguerite and I lived in five different places.

Jane and I lived in Nevada five years, in Oregon five, in Spokane nine, in Baltimore seven, one in Maine, and ten in Ellicott City. We moved to Vantage House in November 2003. I will be here twelve years in November 2015. For Jane and me, this somewhat nomadic life brought changes that were never unwelcome, and each seemed to have its own adventures, its own challenges, and its own good memories. Parting from friends was difficult, but their warmth and caring followed us and filled our new life with precious memories. I think I'm finally in a house where I can say, "I'll be here the rest of my life."

*

There was only one move Jane and I made that we regretted. In 1993, I grew restless or listless, either of which was an unusual experience for me. I'm not sure what it was. I was seventy-four and maybe I was having a "change of life" experience of some sort. I began to talk about retiring and moving. Where to go? We talked to our best friends, Morris and Priscilla Scherr, and asked them what area they would like best of all to move to if they had their choice.

They said, "Maine."

We had been in Maine for a week's vacation the summer prior to this conversation. I began talking to Jane about a move to Maine.

We discussed the possibility over a period of time and Jane expressed agreement. We always talked things over openly and at length, and our natural compatibility was never shaken during any decisions we made. Over the course of a few weeks, Maine became a serious consideration, pending a final decision. We decided to have another look and went for a week's vacation to Maine.

It was a fateful decision. We saw a few houses and when we saw our first post-and-beam house we fell in love with it. It was truly a fascinating house with striking exposed beams and the posts that held them up, a modern and somewhat elegant kitchen, and a large stone fireplace. The yard stretched down to the St. George River, an estuary. We thought and talked about it overnight and purchased it the next morning before we left for Baltimore. In retrospect, perhaps Jane was more enthusiastic about the house than she was about Maine. Jane loved houses. As I reflect, I believe her love for the house was a major factor in why I wanted to buy it *for her*.

After the move, I worked halftime at the local Mental Health Clinic, the only psychiatrist in the immediate area. It was a lonely time for Jane. To get our mail, she walked to the St. George Post Office, a little shack of a place about two hundred yards away. Before long they closed it permanently. Jane went to shops in nearby Rockland but found shoppers and shopkeepers not especially warm toward "an outsider." As usual, we spent all our free time together. We walked the ocean beaches and along the river. We got outfitted for cross-country skiing and enjoyed the experience.

Several family members and friends came to visit us. Jane's younger daughter, Bonnie, came with her husband in a small plane he rented and flew. My older son, Bob, came, and John, my middle son, came up a couple of times. And as I mentioned, Paul and Sharlene visited and we were reunited. Laura and her husband also visited. On their vacation, two priests whom we had known for years stopped by for a couple of days. But Jane seemed sad at times and not her usual self.

We visited our friends Morris and Priscilla in Baltimore.

Morris asked, "Are you happy in Maine, Janie?"

Jane bluntly answered, "No."

On the drive back to Maine, I asked Jane if she would like to move back to the Baltimore area. Of course she would. Later, I saw some of the notes she had written during the time in Maine. She was clearly getting depressed; and as commonly happens with a depressed person's thinking, Jane thought the door was closed on doing something about the situation. She thought we were doomed to live out our lives in Maine. Since I seemed to be happy there, she was happy for me. But she was not happy for her and that would have made me unhappy. We needed to leave.

•

After fourteen months there, we returned to Maryland and bought a house in Ellicott City. Deep down I suspect Jane never wanted to go to Maine in the first place, but she "got on board" in order to please me. That was Jane's love, to be concerned about my welfare, my desires. Was it all a mistake? Living in Ellicott City markedly changed our life as opposed to living in Baltimore. The ten years in Ellicott City were good years and of course concluded with our providential move to Vantage House.

I returned to work at Taylor Manor Hospital in Ellicott City and I returned to the adjunct faculty at Loyola University. When Taylor Manor Hospital was sold, I left and started a private practice in Ellicott City which continued until December 2005.

Chapter Ten:
A Lost and Found World

If you recently walked the wooded pathways near Vantage House, you will realize how much the scenery has changed. The sight and sound of traffic, large buildings, and residential homes are hidden from view by the lush growth of a well-watered spring. It's almost hard to believe those bare sticks that stood tall, stark and silent now have a sound of their own and screen from view another world.

We are not surprised each time the world changes in familiar ways, changes we have lived through so many times. Spring and summer, fall and winter follow the calendar schedule with their own variation. But there is a reassuring certainty in their coming. There is a special pleasure in the first flowers, the birthing leaves, the robin's return, the goslings newly introduced to life. And six months from now we'll hear the crackle of dying leaves and look for the purity of newly fallen snow. In the turn of seasons, nature repeats the lessons of holding and letting go, finding and releasing, seeking and losing.

But lessons of the world around us seem not to translate easily into lessons for the world within us. With aging, we are no longer "people of all seasons." We find, we seek, and we hold. Letting go, losing, and releasing is something we rarely accept willingly or do gracefully.

Newly arrived residents are buried in a world of loss: the home they left behind, the possessions they couldn't bring, the street, and the neighborhood where they lived. And that's only the beginning. There is the seemingly endless problem of items that were packed and now can't be found. How many of us who have lived here for years can't find the items we "put somewhere just a few days ago!"

Over time, we all develop a fear of "what will I lose next?" Of course, it isn't primarily *things* we fear losing. It is people, family, friends— those who cradled our presence and those with whom we lived the life we hold so closely in our hearts. Each time something can't be found or someone is temporarily unavailable the pain of past loss overwhelms us. Brief desperation may fill us for a moment.

The stars that shone for life's conquests dimmed long ago as our careers faded into the mists of aging. And now deep within there is a growing awareness of losing bits and pieces of ourselves: the vigor, the interest, the determination of the past, and the *joie de vivre*. Curiosity has narrowed its perspective. Enthusiasm has grown lethargic.

"Letting go" is not really a new experience. We've been doing it throughout our lives, sometimes painfully, sometimes joyfully, and sometimes proudly. We gave up the immaturity of adolescence. We let go of decisions we might have made or paths we might have walked. We lost some of the habits whether good or bad. We released some of the bitterness over unhappy events, and some of the misgivings over choices we made.

Nature teaches, "For all things there is a season." Now is the season to hold onto small things still within our reach, still within our reason: a kind word to a friend, a smile and word of greeting (names not necessary), an awareness of some goodness each day brings, gratitude for what we have and for those who still are of significance in our lives. The goodness of our lives, those who nurtured the goodness, and those who shared it with us will never be lost. **Goodness** is never out of season.

+ + + + + + + + + +

I've mentioned that in 1971 we left Reno and moved to Grants Pass, Oregon. I was the only psychiatrist living in Josephine County. Medford was about thirty miles away and had three or four psychiatrists and a psychiatric unit at the local hospital. I had a halftime position at the Grants Pass Mental Health Clinic. In addition, I started a private practice in a one bedroom house we bought and Jane and I remodeled to make a very comfortable office.

I would guess the population in Grants Pass at that time was about fifteen to twenty thousand. Fortunately, my office was not on a main street and did have off-street parking, making it less likely that one would be seen "going to the psychiatrist." This was still a time when psychiatric care might stir doubts about those in such need. The practice was established rather quickly. It was in that location, Howard, the man I referred to earlier, first came to see me. Actually, he lived in Medford, but his smoldering paranoia probably motivated him to seek treatment in Grants Pass.

My position as the only psychiatrist in town was helpful. It brought me into some forensic work, primarily evaluations of persons facing charges, and then court testimony. I learned from the experience the report I wrote would be used in court by the attorney only if it was favorable to the client. If it was unfavorable, of course it never got into the hands of the prosecution. Our next door neighbor was an attorney and we became friends with him and his family and with his partner.

•

I usually saw patients at the Mental Health Clinic only by appointments arranged with the secretary who made up the schedule. One day during our lunch period, a woman walked in and said she needed to see the psychiatrist as soon as possible. I finished my lunch and told the secretary I would see the woman in my office.

When Kate came in and sat down, after introductions I opened the conversation with one of my usual openings: "What brings you in to see me today?"

Her reply, "I just killed my husband."

Without need of prompting, she continued her story. The couple was in their early thirties, had been married about six years and had no children. They had been physically active, hiking, white-water rafting, mountain climbing, motorcycling and so on. About three years ago, the husband fell during a climb resulting in a spinal cord injury and lower body paralysis. For the past year or more, he begged her to shoot and kill him. She felt extremely sad about his condition and began to dread those days when he would plead for release from it all. That very day they were sitting in the sun outside their house. Her husband began weeping and begging her to kill him. She went in the house, got a gun, came out, and shot him. She said she felt like she was someone else when she pulled the trigger. She left him there by the house and came directly to the clinic. She was calm during the interview, spoke in a monotone, and showed little emotion. I thought she was trying desperately to avoid hysteria.

I asked her if I could call an attorney I knew and ask his advice. She agreed. I called my attorney-neighbor and his partner responded. He asked me to send her to his office and he would inform the police. After talking with her the attorney took her to the police station and she was arrested.

A few days after her arrest, the attorney asked me to do a formal psychiatric evaluation of Kate. There was no family history of psychiatric illness nor was there any evidence of mental illness other than the depression and anxiety, which began subsequent to her husband's injury. Kate was alert and cooperative during the evaluation and was assessed as having average or above average intelligence. There was no evidence of disturbed thought process or content. Affect was flat but appropriate. Mood was moderately depressed relative to her husband's severe impairment and the continuing impact it had on both of them. She had been sleeping poorly for several weeks prior to the murder. She reported feeling overwhelmed by the reality of her husband's severely limited life, and his tearful pleading brought her to submit to what he begged her to do.

I found no evidence of severe mental illness, but reported her moderately depressed state of mind over the past three years. Although her thought process was not severely impaired, it was, to say the least, influenced by her husband's repeated pleading to die. My conclusion was Kate was moderately depressed at the time of the murder, she knew the difference between right and wrong at the time, but her act occurred at a time of moderately impaired judgment due to her mental state.

I remember my own feelings during the time of my court testimony. As a psychiatrist, I felt deeply sympathetic for Kate. There was ample evidence besides her word, this was a couple truly devoted to each other, enjoying an active life together, and then struck down by his crippling accident. And now Kate had to live, not just with the loss of her life partner, but with the horrible fact she had killed him. I had difficulty not showing my own emotion during my testimony.

I had confronted the district attorney a couple of times in prior cases. He was a rather pompous individual and had the habit of asking questions with lengthy and wandering introductions. On two or three occasions when he produced his extended and tedious questioning and relinquished the floor for an answer, I would ask:

"Would you mind repeating the question?" I knew it irritated him and interfered with his line of thought.

I've mellowed since those days. I've repented all the vengeful things I've done in the past and try sincerely to avoid any vengeful behavior in the present. It disturbs me when that old sense of "getting even" stares me in the face over some trivial thing (or even serious thing) someone does. "Vengeance is mine," says the Lord.

Once the case was given to the jury, Kate's attorney and Jane and I retired to our house to await the verdict. It seems strange to me now to remember we sat drinking coffee while this woman's fate was being decided. After about three hours, the attorney received the phone call and we returned to the courthouse. Kate was found guilty and sentenced to twenty years in the state penitentiary.

The story does not end there. About two years later, Kate's attorney called and asked if I would accompany him to the penitentiary. Kate was due to come up before the parole board in a few months. We went to see her. She had been a model prisoner since admission. I did another psychiatric evaluation and based on current findings was able to write a letter on her behalf to the parole board. When she was paroled about one year after that visit, we were no longer in Grants Pass, so I didn't get to see her on her return.

•

We left Grants Pass the summer of 1976. An impulsive decision? Well, no. We had thought about it for a year or more. Thinking about it had really been forced on us. The court in Reno had finally decided to hear Marguerite's case to collect past due alimony. There was a hearing in Reno. We visited our good friends, Tom Craven and his wife, while we were there. When Tom learned which judge heard the case, he predicted we wouldn't get a decision for several years. It turned out to be two years and it was unfavorable for me. With interest included, the bill was somewhere around two or three hundred thousand dollars.

•

By this time, we had bought another house on the Oregon coast. This was truly a dream house. It sat on fifteen acres of land overlooking the beach without public access but half a mile off the coastal highway. The owner had a right-away across the private land going to the house. It was built with precious Port Orford cedar, had radiant heating throughout, two large fireplaces, one in the kitchen-dining area, and the other in the living room. Four bedrooms, two and a half baths, an enclosed garage, and a deck overlooking the ocean—a dream house in a dream location!

We came on it quite accidently. We would often go to our Nesika Beach house on weekends and we would attend the Catholic Church in Gold Beach. We dealt with the local hardware dealer for things we needed at our Nesika Beach house (the $20,000 one). He knew Jane loved to look at houses. One Sunday after Mass, he said he had a friend who was building a rather unique house in Gold Beach. Would we like to see it? Could we do otherwise?

We saw the house that was nearing completion. It was impressive. The owner mentioned he was selling their house up the road at Ophir (ten or fifteen miles north of Gold Beach). The price sounded reasonable. We wanted to see it. We bought it. Now we had four mortgages in Oregon.

•

A couple of years after that purchase we faced the court order for delinquent alimony. We discussed our situation with our attorney friend and asked him what might happen if we did not respond to the court order.

He said, "You may come home from work one day and find a moving truck loaded with your furniture and a lock on your door."

Disconcerting to say the least. It started us thinking about where to go to avoid this mountain of debt crashing down on our heads.

As an aside, and to explain my reaction: I believed the alimony was an unjust debt based on the original document I signed in order to be released from jail in Maryland. My first wife and her attorney had been devious and deceitful in not coming forward to respond to my request for a divorce. I considered the original *ne exeiat* order invalid because, in fact, I was not abandoning my first wife and children without provisions for their welfare.

Jane and I even thought of moving to Canada. For Christmas, we went to see Don and Helen on the ranch. We talked to one of my cousins who owned a bank in a nearby town. We stashed about $30,000 with him but that was a drop in the alimony bucket. And our bucket was not very full.

•

Going home after Christmas, we always went through Spokane and this time we decided to look at houses there. We always thought Spokane looked like a nice town and it was nearer the ranch and our closest family. A realtor showed us several. Of course, we found another dream house. It had a rich brown wainscoting in the living room, entrance hall and dining room with large boxed beams in their ceilings. We bought it that day. We do sound a little wacky I guess when it comes to houses, and one would think we had a few million dollars lying around somewhere. Now we had five mortgages with the threat of the court taking all of it, because there certainly wasn't much cash to take.

Part of our reasoning was to liquidate the houses in Oregon and put the cash somewhere safe. Where? The court would demand to know where it went. Perjury? Certainly not! We were not being terribly wise. It's amazing how the mind can come up with ridiculous answers when one is feeling boxed in and quite helpless. In reality it seemed like we were somehow just trying to delay the inevitable. We sold the four houses in Oregon fairly readily and made a fair profit on them all.

We left some very good friends in Oregon, but we weren't sad to leave. During the previous winter, we had not seen the sun from late October until late February. Grants Pass was noted for having the lowest mean wind velocity in the U.S. But one year the fog settled in the bowl of hills and mountains surrounding the town and it just stayed there. We visited friends who lived on one of the hills. They had nice sunny days most of the winter.

•

The first house we bought in Oregon, the Nesika Beach house, became an office, which helped the income tax burden. Once a month, I consulted at the Mental Health Center in Gold Beach. As a result, I obtained two or three private referrals, patients I would see in the Nesika Beach house when we came to work on the Ophir house on weekends. Yes, I said "work" because once more there were "modifications" to make. I removed a free-standing wall separating the kitchen from the dining room. The ceiling of the enlarged space sloped upward from nine feet on the kitchen wall to thirteen feet on the dining room wall. We painted most of the rooms and made a brick deck on the shady side of the house.

I need to emphasize something about this period in our life. There was never one time Jane and I disagreed or had an argument about what we planned to do. We were both anxious and deeply concerned about how and when the alimony and court orders would eventually be resolved. We thought it through together and made our decisions as one.

I did additional psychiatric evaluations in Grants Pass for local attorneys. Several evaluations were of murderers. Cave Junction was a small town less than an hour from Grants Pass. We drove through it coming and going to Gold Beach. It harbored many persons "of the LSD and free-love age." It had become something of a haven for those who abandoned the Haight-Asbury region of California when the law began to interfere with their "hippie" lifestyle. Among the frequent minor crimes occurring in Cave Junction, one major crime stood out. Two young men were arrested for beheading a man and his wife with a machete on some isolated road not far from town.

I evaluated Frank, one of the two. He was in his early twenties, ordinary looking, cooperative, and of at least average intelligence. I don't remember most of the details. He acknowledged he and his companion were both "high" on a variety of drugs. (LSD was especially popular at that time). Their intent was to rob the couple. He said his partner began acting "strange", waving the machete around and finally striking and killing the man with it. Then he ordered Frank to kill the woman. In his frenzied state, he threatened to kill Frank unless he complied. Frank killed the women and together they cut off the two heads.

My report found a cooperative, intelligent, emotionally composed, and coherent young man accused of murder. There was a history of extensive substance abuse, but no history of serious mental illness in the accused or his family, as far as family history was known. The report stated he knew the difference between right and wrong at the time of the act and knew the act was wrong. There was evidence of diminished capacity at the time of the crime because of excessive substance abuse and possibly because of fear related to the alleged threat from his companion. I was not called to testify because my findings would not have been of value to the defense attorney.

There was another case of diminished capacity I evaluated in Grants Pass. The man was a Native American who was drinking in a local bar. There was an argument between him and another bar customer. A fight ensued and during the fight the Native American drew a knife and killed the other man. The Native American was a heavy drinker, was clearly intoxicated, and had been provoked. I reported diminished capacity due to intoxication. He was found not guilty, a verdict which surprised me a bit.

There was a fourth murderer I was asked to evaluate. It was a gruesome crime. A man and woman had stopped for the night at a local motel. The next morning, after the man vacated the room, the maid found the woman hanging from the shower rod and butchered as one would butcher a deer, hanging with her head down and cut open from pelvis to throat. Obviously, one could assume powerful psychiatric issues had been involved.

After the man was in jail for a day or two, he was taken to the psychiatric unit in Medford. I was asked by the county attorney to see him there. I visited him and obtained no useful information. His voice was a mumble and wandered from subject to subject without rationality. He denied any knowledge of the crime. I suggested we consider a sodium amytal interview to see if we might obtain some coherent information. The county attorney and the man's court appointed attorney agreed. One of the Medford psychiatrists agreed to assist me. The "truth serum" interview was of no value. I had no follow-up on the case so my assumption was he was transferred to the Oregon State Mental Hospital in Salem for further evaluation and treatment.

•

Cave Junction was the source of several "welfare" evaluations I did for the Social Security Administration. The "hippies" from San Francisco did not fare too well in this rural sector of Oregon partly because of their continued substance abuse and petty crime. Few of them were able to find employment in the area.

A young woman came for such an evaluation. At one time she had been a successful employee of a jewelry store in California. Her mother was deceased and she had lived with her father in the San Francisco area. He was a successful business man. She began using LSD and lost her job as a result. Her relationship with her father deteriorated because of her substance abuse. He grew increasingly concerned about her. They quarreled. She packed up a few belongings and with some friends moved to Cave Junction leaving no information for her father. She was an intelligent, responsive young woman and straight forward in answering questions. Her mood was mildly dysphoric, but affect was bright. She had successfully discontinued substance abuse and she had a positive attitude about her future.

I saw her as a good candidate for some therapy sessions and suggested she consider it. She was clearly making an effort to get her life on a better level, but currently had no one to support her in the endeavor. She responded she would like to come for therapy but could not afford it. I agreed to see her every two weeks over a short period without charge. She did well in therapy as we reviewed her family background, her various family relationships, her earlier aspirations, and her pathway into substance abuse. She was intelligent, sensitive, and rather quickly developed some insight into the brighter as well as the darker aspects of her life.

She talked about her father with deep affection. I encouraged her to contact him, which she eventually did. He came to visit her and together they discussed her plans for the future and her return to San Francisco. I arranged for our last appointment. During the visit she gave me a necklace "for your wife." It was on a simple neck band holding an attached large dark greenish stone (possibly jade or opal) with a band of gold wrapped twice around the stone to hold it. It was absolutely beautiful and certainly unique. She made it! When Jane wore it, people often commented on its beauty. It was outstanding! Years later, we were getting a professional evaluation on some jewelry and I sent the necklace along. It was evaluated at $1,500.00. Laura now has the necklace.

I was generously paid for the time I spent with this woman. Payment was not just the totally unexpected necklace, but of greater value was the satisfaction I got from the reunion of this gentle, caring young woman with the father who thought she was lost to him forever. Undoubtedly, my lost relationship with my youngest son entered into my emotional exposure at the time.

•

One might question why my feelings were so involved in my relationship with this patient. My feelings were part of my relationship with all my patients. If I didn't have feelings related to what they were telling me about themselves, their lives, their family, their friends, their work, their comings and goings, I would not be fully able to understand them. When I came to know, yes, almost to feel what they were experiencing or had experienced, then I could work with them. It felt like I was temporarily, not just an onlooker, but a partner in their experience of life and its significant events.

Teaching students to be counselors, I used to tell them: If you have patients you don't like, get to know them better. You don't yet know them well enough, because when you truly get to know them and *why* they are *how* they are, then you will like them.

In my spiritual world, I imagine God as "The Great Psychiatrist." In God's psychiatric role, God not only knows us, but knows all the little things that entered into our mistakes and the wrong paths we travelled.

When we say, "How could I have done that? Why was I so foolish? What was wrong with me?" God knows all the details, the feelings, the enticements, and the weaknesses. With that kind of understanding on God's part, I pray for forgiveness. When a psychiatrist even approaches that depth with a patient, they both have understanding. Security and stability are just a step away.

Do therapists have favorites? Of course, they do. Unless they are "stick of wood" therapists, and there are such. But if the therapist is an emotionally responsive person (which in my judgment is a *sine qua non* to be a good therapist), then they will have favorites *but* they will not treat them any differently than their other patients.

I think most professional persons have favorites, the same as clerks in stores, restaurateurs, and school bus drivers do. The same as most persons with adequate emotional quotients do. Perhaps it is only those on the low end of the emotional quotient scale who don't have favorites. They treat everyone the same—as objects.

So, what do therapists do with all these feelings which invade the inner sanctum of their mind? Leave them in the office? Easier said than done. I think every therapist should have a human sounding board to bounce their feelings against. They need a person to talk to about all the "stuff" they bring home in their head and especially in their heart.

My social work students back in the sixties and my pastoral counseling students in eighties and nineties would tell me they could not reveal to anyone (other than their supervisor) things patients talk about during a therapy session. It is all confidential material! Sort of like the seal of the confessional for Catholic priests. But I have often heard priests referring to what some totally unidentified person at some totally unspecified time said in the confessional. In my judgment, the same arrangement applies to a therapist. The confidante should not know the person and should have no way of connecting comments to any particular person.

The "sounding board" concept is important to the well-being of the therapist. It's a little like the need to unload the burden of a significant event by getting it out into words someone can hear, whether or not they decide to respond. I regularly talked to Jane about episodes in the office that were particularly emotional for me or those that seemed to be highlighted somewhere inside my head. She might or might not respond. It was said. Someone heard me. That was all I needed. I mentioned earlier it would be a handicap for me to return to private practice and not have Jane to be my sounding board.

In fact, Jane plays that part for me even now. If something has annoyed or disturbed me, I mention it out loud to Jane when I get back to my apartment. In the old days, she would usually comment, but sometimes not. She never comments now, but I know she hears me. That's all I need is someone to hear me.

Chapter Eleven:
Retirement: A Road Last Travelled

Psychiatrists spend years helping others confront the personal experiences and life events that dishevel their emotions, disrupt their plans, distort their intentions and batter their lives. We remain observant and professionally detached as patients explore all aspects of life in the recounted histories of the hurting, confused, misguided, and mismatched who come to us. We hear all the stories there are to tell of abuse, neglect, and indulgence; stories of love and hate, of goodness and violence, and of life and of death. We provide care on the premise that change can and will come and life will be better.

All this work and gradual growth consumes *time*, a key issue in therapy. We attend to time as a scheduling issue and as a necessary ingredient to successful therapy. We often recommend the value of "free time" to patients as a part of successful therapy. And all the while, our own "free time" becomes increasingly precious and its diminishment nags us quietly, but persistently. "Free time" becomes a luxury in the busyness of life. Ah! The quietude! The peace! The freedom in that little space of existence that is our very own!

In the rush of busy practice, we become "clock watchers" and find ourselves focusing on "saving time," as if it could be stored away somewhere and its later availability would allow fulfillment of all those dreams of travelling, reading, long walks, and enjoying life.

Then comes retirement! Comes freedom! Comes leisure! Prolonged waiting is ended. Our time-treasure lies before us. It is ours to spend as we please.

Comes the unpleasant awareness, "free time" is not as "free" as we expected. There are obligations and responsibilities. Various life-items need to be decided, managed, and monitored. Rarely is time as easily controlled in retirement as it was in our practice-world. Accommodations are required. Schedules involve the needs and decisions of others. Personal conflicts occur in the face of new and complex interactions with those whose lives now intersect more frequently with our own: wives, children, friends, colleagues, and neighbors.

We spent years helping others accommodate to relational complexities by mollifying responses and modifying behaviors. Now our own difficulty doing what we so readily recommended may create discord. This "introductory phase" to retirement is usually unexpected, sometimes difficult, rarely "a wash." It may require some "intrapersonal counseling." We are now, in a sense, on the other side of the desk.

And some dreams do come true. Items on the "bucket list" are scratched off after the grand cruise, various trips, a regular golf schedule, books that needed to be read, a fill of favorite restaurants, regular gym, some operas, Broadway shows, tennis lessons, and upgrading the house.

Undoubtedly, the most challenging sector of retirement is aging. It is more often faced with anxiety than with grace. It hangs on the fringes of life for a while: wrinkles come, hair goes, new aches and pains, slight physical limitations (button holes seem smaller), shirts and blouses, pants and skirts a bit larger, immediate memory a bit slower. All not worrisome yet, but annoying and disconcerting. The internist begins to ask and then to show concern about cholesterol, blood pressure, unsteadiness, blood sugar, etc. Questions about diet and exercise are not reassuring. They get our attention which is exactly why they are asked. Changes are recommended far more often than they are followed.

As life goes on, the years seem to pass quickly but the days drag wearisomely. We "time watchers" are puzzled by this seeming change. The stark truth: clocks tick to the same rhythm all over the world, but the music of life is not *legato*. Eventually, we find ourselves "time-wealthy," wondering how to spend our late life treasure which unexpectedly presents now as less alluring, less gracious. Old age intrudes boldly and often brazenly into our world and begins stealthily, but steadily, not only to reduce our stores of time, but with unseemliness to limit our ability to spend what remains in our account.

Finally we learn what we always wanted our patients to understand. You remember the words: "Things can change and do change, you know. And there *will be an end to this particular struggle you're having.*"

+ + + + + + + + +

The above article was published in *Psychiatric News* July 25, 2014. It is the psychiatric alternative to "About Time," the article that opened the first chapter of this book. So yes, it should sound familiar. The editor of *Psychiatric News* read "About Time" and asked me if I could do something similar for the News.

I chose this article now partly because the previous pages brought it to mind. I believe the ideas presented are also applicable to most professional men and women who "can't wait to retire." After retirement, the question often becomes: "what will I do with my time?" Those who worked in trades such as plumbing, carpentry, air conditioning, and jobs requiring physical abilities and skills have more "puttering potential" than others and can do just that with continuing interest and satisfaction. Retired professionals are more likely to find activities which fill their time, but not their need to be of value in the world or to have a sense of personal accomplishment. Winning a golf game or taking a cruise hardly fulfills more significant needs. Volunteering is a useful outlet and something I was eager to do in my own field. *But* I no longer have a medical license or malpractice insurance, or Jane, all of which closes the door on volunteering in mental health.

One of the highlights of my current life is to spend ninety minutes each week "supervising" a social work friend of mine. I don't really see it as supervision. We discuss some of her more interesting and sometimes more challenging clients. During that all too brief time, it feels like I'm back in the office tracking down the persons who or the events which were so damaging to each of the clients we discuss. It's next best to being in my own office, and of course, I have no rent to pay, no bills to send, and no managed care to trouble me. But no income from it!

There are professionals who never found a sense of accomplishment, much less excitement in their work. They are the ones who had the education, earned the degrees, and felt too strongly the expectations of family and friends. What else could they do but continue the profession they regrettably chose? Unfortunately, that regret may have remained a negative factor throughout their professional life. I have, on occasion, treated professionals who clearly were doing something that had little meaning for them other than making a living. It showed.

To see people who obviously enjoy what they do has always been a pleasure for me. Even though they get caught up in difficult times or confront serious problems, nothing in their manner detracts from the evidence of dedication. Some of the most troubling patients I had were those who were dedicated and enjoyed their work but their firm or company became increasingly demanding of time and effort as a result of company downsizing. Their lifetime career was jeopardized because of the strain. Their age usually added to their conflict. They were in their fifties or early sixties not a good age to start looking for another position. The firm's message was typically:

"If you can't keep up with the work, we'll get someone *younger* who can."

The word "younger" was never spoken, but was obviously in the atmosphere. It was important to avoid age discrimination. "The company" exists to make money not to take care of the elderly.

I can honestly and heartily say, "I loved being a psychiatrist." I felt I was born to be one. It was a bit like I had envisioned the priesthood but without the celibacy. It was rewarding in so many ways and opened up a world of possibilities for me. The best part was doing psychotherapy. All my patients were interesting to me. It sometimes took time for me to realize how interesting they were, but they were persons of value the moment they entered my office. I often compared being a therapist to being a detective. I started with the assumption someone or something had harmed them in some way. It was my job to help them find the damaging event or relationship and help them mend their mental wounds.

As I write this, I wonder about the individuals I saw who had committed murder. Comments in the above paragraph would also describe my perspective toward each of them. But what if I had seen the mortally shot husband, the woman killed with a butcher knife, the beheaded couple, or the woman hanging like a butchered deer? Would I then have been able to maintain my objectivity toward them, or would the view of their victims have contaminated my impartiality? I can only assume such a viewing or vivid description of the victims often contaminates the objectivity of the police, the press, and jurors.

In addition to the satisfaction I found in private practice, I had the wonderful opportunity to enter the world of administration in Reno. Later, I was the Director of the Isaac Taylor Institute of Psychiatry and Religion at Taylor Manor Hospital in Ellicott City, MD. I had that position for approximately three years before Jane and I moved to Maine.

•

Based on my background in psychiatry and psychology, I also had the opportunity to lecture and give workshops in over 50% of the contiguous states. These programs were typically at the request of Catholic religious communities of men or women. The most interesting and challenging program of this kind occurred in 1964 and 1965. The program was conducted for the public in a Catholic parish hall in New York City. It was billed as: "A Dialogue between a Priest and a Psychiatrist." There were seven talks in the series, one every Wednesday evening during Lent. The priest was Father Rover, a Dominican from Boston.

Every Wednesday, Father Rover flew down from Boston and I flew up from D.C. In those days, Eastern Airways had shuttle planes between Washington and New York. I think they were scheduled every hour during rush hours. You could walk on board without a reservation and you could buy your ticket on board. Of course, there were no inspection stations to pass through in those days. It was like running to catch a bus. Someone would meet me at the airport (Newark, I think) and take me to the host parish. I would have dinner, say, "Hello," to Father Rover, and we were on stage.

We had a publicized topic for each talk. Father Rover and I never communicated with one another about the topic or what each was prepared to say. We seemed to have a natural rapport, a comfortable connection, and our thoughts and words and minds fit together nicely. The talks went over very well, in fact so well they invited us to return during the following year for another series. It was undoubtedly one of the most exhilarating and novel experiences in my professional life.

•

My educational background gave me teaching opportunities. Teaching was probably the second love of my professional life. I first taught undergraduate students, mostly seminarians, when I was a graduate student at Catholic University. Later, I taught in the Social Work Department at Catholic University, then at Gonzaga University in Spokane, and finally for almost twenty-five years in the Pastoral Counseling Department at Loyola University in Baltimore.

•

I usually saw writing as a side interest, and yet as I review my CV, I find I wrote twenty-four articles in professional and religious journals, and also chapters in four books by other professionals. These writings for the most part dealt with general mental health issues, sometimes focused on religious men and women in the Catholic Church. I also wrote a number of articles and gave lectures related to the emotional struggles and mental health of teenagers.

My first book was published in 1969, *Conflict in Community*, St. John's University Press, Collegeville, MN. It sold very well, perhaps because it appeared shortly after Vatican II. At that time there were growing concerns within religious communities about the stability and the future direction of religious life. The book was translated into Spanish and was also published in India. St. John's University Press published the book in a set of six cassettes.

My second book was published by Harper and Row in 1986, *Living the Vows, Emotional Conflicts of Celibate Religious*. By this time, religious men and women faced conflicts, not only in their communities, but in their personal lives and decisions. It was the time when many priests and nuns were leaving the religious life and seeking laicization. Harper and Row did a second printing. This book grew out of the lectures and workshops I had been giving for Catholic religious.

•

As an aside, because of the success of *Living the Vows*, Taylor Manor Hospital started the Isaac Taylor Institute of Psychiatry and Religion and made me the Director. The Institute was an inpatient program for women and men of all faiths who served in a religious role in their church. As patients, they were housed with other patients and were involved in the same therapeutic programs except for their own weekly group therapy session. The program was well publicized with speakers such as M. Scott Peck and Harriet Lerner. We had several nuns, a couple of priests and a number of Protestant ministers as patients. Unfortunately, the program only survived a few years. The Catholic Church seemed to boycott the program as far as their religious were concerned. I will write more about this particular topic later.

•

My third book, *Emotions: Mystery or Madness*, was self-published through AuthorHouse in 2007. By that time, I had left Taylor Manor Hospital and started another private practice. It was a book I believe I wanted to write for a long time and finally was able to do so. It had a satisfactory distribution and found its way into some college and postgraduate programs.

The forensic involvement certainly was a positive experience. It presented me with exaggerated examples of emotions gone astray. It also gave me a limited view "behind the scenes" in courtroom procedures.

Putting this all together now, I realize how many wonderful opportunities I had, how many different people I came in contact with through the years, and how wide a world of emotions and behaviors I encountered. Do I see all these as personal accomplishments? Do I mention them with pride now? Do I boast? In a way, I would say yes to all of those. I am not as humble as I should be, but as I say, yes, I am also quick to realize and acknowledge how much I owe those accomplishments to the long list of people I pray for every day and more centrally to the God who gave me the physical, emotional, and mental health to do whatever I did that was of value to others. I believe I did what I was called to do. My tool box contained the tools. I pray I used them well.

My fourth book was self-published in 2012 through AuthorHouse. It was written during the time of Jane's Alzheimer's illness and was completed after her death in February 2012. It began as an outlet for feelings I could not discuss with Jane and had no desire to share with anyone else. It was a relief and release for me to objectify them in a way by writing them. Jane and I met Harriet Lerner when she lectured at the Isaac Taylor Institute. We kept in touch through the years. I wrote to her about Jane's illness and attached some of the pages I had written. She was the one who prompted me to consider publication. The pages grew through the years and finally became *An Alzheimer's Love Story*. Following publication of the book, I have had a number of opportunities to lecture on the topic of Alzheimer's.

•

In the last chapter, I mentioned we bought a house in Spokane at a time when we were facing a court proceeding to collect past alimony. We moved to Spokane in the summer of 1976. I established an office in a medical building on the north side of town near Holy Family Hospital. I taught at Gonzaga several years and also served as a consultant at the Good Shepard Home for unwed mothers and at a local facility for alcohol and drug addiction.

•

Our daughter, Laura, attended the local Catholic grade school, and then Gonzaga High School where she graduated. A small, but interesting detail: many years earlier all my brothers came from Montana and graduated from Gonzaga High School. My father wanted all of them to have some education in a Jesuit high school.

We made a difficult decision when we moved to Spokane, a decision which, in hindsight, was extremely unfair to our daughter. Jane was exceptionally sensitive about the prevailing attitude that a mother *always* gets the children in a divorce. I think it was more her own sensitivity about the subject than any criticism anyone had ever openly or even indirectly made. No, I do not believe it was a guilty conscience. She knew she did the right thing to leave Tom, right for her, right for her children, and apparently right for him. (His second wife seems to have been a better match). I think Jane continued to mourn the loss of her children. Although her son, Phil, glided in and out of our life through the years, Jane greatly missed her daughters; visits never seemed long enough and correspondence was never satisfying.

So, when we moved to Spokane I suggested to Jane we not tell anyone we both had children from prior marriages. At the time it seemed to be a reasonable thing to do, and Jane readily agreed. In retrospect, it really wasn't a wise choice for either of us. More importantly, we didn't even consider what difficulties it would create for Laura. Essentially, we were asking her to lie about a significant part of her life, as we planned to do. I must admit Jane and I were again thinking of ourselves and what we thought was *best for us*. We had sacrificed our children for our own desires when we left for Nevada, now we were sacrificing Laura's integrity for our desired privacy.

It was also one of those decisions that once you begin the course, there is no way of turning back gracefully. If you tell people the truth later on, will they then doubt your honesty in other things you say? How would you explain the lies? Would they believe the explanation?

It was really my doing. I led, Jane followed. I could try to salvage my ego and say I did it for Jane's sake. It was my dedication to Jane that was at the root of the decision, the same dedication that was with me during the years of her

Alzheimer's disease. But that's a feeble excuse. It was a poor decision whatever reasons I want to try to give myself now. It was unfair to the daughter we loved so much, the one who was our most treasured child because she was *ours*.

An additional sad truth is we never realized how difficult it had been for Laura until a few years ago, when, in an angry moment, Laura referred to it saying how difficult it had been for her to lie to her friends all that time. Of course, children always talk to each other about their siblings. I don't think we ever considered how awkward that might be for her.

She must have wondered about the integrity of her parents. She was in Catholic grade and high school learning it was wrong to lie. At the same time her parents were lying about their lives, and insisting she do the same. We moved to Spokane when Laura was ten and left when she was nineteen—critical years when children learn much from the example of their parents. How could she not wonder about our sense of values and our veracity as she sorted through the experiences of those years developing her own moral compass?

One never knows how something like that influences situations and decisions later in life. I can't help but wonder how our dishonesty of those years touched Laura's life. I am grateful to see her now as a woman of remarkable integrity. The knowledge I have gained by this reflection casts a dark cloud over my thoughts of Spokane and the nine years we spent there. This was one of the few decisions I truly wish I could undo, but the bell was rung and the echo will always be inside my head and my heart.

Of course, it was easier for Jane and me to say what we had agreed to say. *We* did not have other children. Of course, Laura could have used a similar deceptive phrase and said she had no *siblings*; they were all half-siblings. Before we left Spokane we told our friends about our *other children*. I don't think anyone was shocked by the news, and by that time they knew us well enough not to question our conduct or decisions of the past.

•

We moved to Spokane with an alimony debt still looming in our future. The Ophir Beach house was a rather unique sale. The wife of the couple who bought the house insisted we include all the furniture in the house, for an additional charge of course. Fortunately, all the articles were for weekend use and not part of Jane's treasured pieces. We set the date to complete the sale. When I left the house that morning to go to the office, there was a note on the windshield of my pick-up. The woman wanted to buy it too. The sale went through but I kept my truck.

The house at Nesika Beach was sold to our best friends for a small amount more than we paid for it. He was in the mobile home business. He later moved a mobile home onto the outer lot by the beach, and then sold the inner lot with the house. We received a picture from them several years later. The soft bank was regularly battered by coastal storms and the soil erosion was so severe the mobile home partially fell over the cliff and became unsalvageable.

•

We found an excellent attorney in Spokane, Bob Crotty. Shortly after we started working with him, he called and said he could not be our attorney. His firm also included a Portland, Oregon office. All the firm's attorneys had just met together and discussed clients. Marguerite was a client in the Portland office. He referred us to a colleague. We met with the colleague and were equally delighted with him. Within a couple of weeks of our meeting, I picked up the morning paper; the attorney died of a heart attack the previous day. Sometime later we went to his associate and were not pleased with his response. We kept delaying any further decisions about it all.

After a year or more, we called Bob Crotty again to get another referral. He checked with his firm. There had been no further action in the Portland office, so the firm decided he could take our case. Another godsend in our life! Bob was diligent and gave the matter a great deal of attention. He contacted Marguerite's attorney in Maryland. In fact, he had been in Maryland on other business and paid Marguerite a visit. The attorneys agreed to take the case to a Spokane judge for settlement. No one was called to testify. The Spokane judge found that the original agreement I signed in the Maryland jail was *unconscionable* and denied the claim for past alimony. The year was 1984. You can be sure I include Bob Crotty in my daily prayers.

Chapter Twelve: The Five Minute Hour

Psychiatry has greatly changed in the past sixty years, and one might ask how much the change has modified patient care. This paper recounts some of the writer's personal experiences with the stark and radical alterations that have occurred.

A residency in the late fifties under the guidance of Dr. Leo Bartemeier introduced me to his masterful ability to elicit the significant and impactful details of a patient's life. Leo was a prominent psychiatric leader, indeed one of the great men of that psychiatric era. He firmly believed every psychiatrist in training should undergo analysis. It was a minor thorn for him I did not do so.

We were trained in what one would now consider classical psychiatric practice. Patients had appointments at least once a week for "the fifty-minute hour." The ten-minute break was to write some notes, review the chart before the next patient and attend to personal needs. That was the framework on which we were to piece together the patient's significant history as Leo looked over our shoulder, so to speak, in weekly supervision. We spent three years doing fifty-minute sessions and sorting through the detritus of childhood years, the ashes of lost relationships, the turmoil of current emotions, and all the connecting links.

The first significant psychiatric medicine of the twentieth century, chlorpromazine hydrochloride, came into use in the late fifties. But with or without it, people got well and with time and therapy went home. Discharge depended on improvement and improvement depended primarily on psychotherapy. At that time, Managed Care Organizations (MCO's) were not managing treatment from a far off business watchtower.

After thirty plus years of practice, in the late nineties I began working half-time in the outpatient department of a psychiatric hospital. I was assigned some patients who were involved in therapy with other professional counselors. I would not prescribe for them unless I saw them for twenty-five-minute segments with a frequency I felt their medications and condition required. The program director was not pleased and insisted I should see six patients every hour for "med management." I soon returned to private practice providing psychotherapy and medication as needed in fifty-minute segments. Patients referred for medication by other therapists were never seen for less than twenty-five minutes and with suitable frequency.

In our present society, many people disdainfully describe psychiatrists as "pill pushers." Many currently practicing psychiatrists prescribe medicines for patients from whom they have never taken a thorough and detailed life history. Patient visits last approximately five minutes at varying intervals. In some cases, medications are prescribed by nurse practitioners during five to ten minute visits, and some patients never have a full psychiatric evaluation. Some of them are not even referred for psychotherapy to any provider.

A recent study published in *JAMA Psychiatry* reported that data from sixty-three general hospitals over a three year period showed an estimated 89,094 annual Emergency Department visits for adverse events related to the use of psychiatric medications, with about one in five patients requiring hospital admission. Is this costly statistic possibly related to the "five-minute hour?"

Doctors and patients are advised "to choose wisely" in the use of psychiatric medicines. A *wise* choice can only be made after a detailed life history provides familiarity not only with the trauma of earlier years, but the scars that remain and continue to impact every day function. Medicines do not alleviate the undeserved shame and guilt from sexual abuse nor the secret fears and smoldering hostility from physical abuse. Emotions are not just chemical changes that can be wiped away or deadened with "wisely chosen" medicines.

I taught and worked with social workers, psychologists and pastoral counselors. Generally, they appear to be not thoroughly trained in the delicate art of probing and making insightful associations which open the inner shell of the patient and expose first the chaos and finally the pearl of self.

Whatever medicines are discovered, whatever techniques of brain invasion are developed, "talking therapy" will still be missing for those in need of words to calm the turmoil deep within, to restore their faith in self, and to conclude they are still of value. Talk is cheap, *listening is not.* So who will listen?

+ + + + + + + + + +

I submitted the above article to the *Psychiatric News* several months ago. It was not rejected, but neither was it printed. I really did not expect it to be accepted. It is a rather harsh and perhaps narrow view of the psychiatric profession as now practiced.

The art of listening is rarely part of the armamentarium of contemporary psychiatrists. The invasion of Managed Care markedly limits payment rates for therapy sessions. Payments for "medication management" remain reasonable. Under Managed Care income for psychiatrists doing therapeutic sessions is less than a fifth of the income for psychiatrists doing medication management. Psychiatrists who want to continue doing psychotherapy generally drop out of the Managed Care market and charge fees which most people cannot afford.

These changes left the field of talk therapy primarily in the domain of social workers, psychologists, and pastoral counselors who do not have the medical background and training comparable to that of psychiatrists. When these counselors see persons for therapy, they may well be concerned about presenting symptoms and are likely to wonder about the benefit of medications. To resolve their doubts and to protect themselves from malpractice claims, they are prone to refer many of their patients to a psychiatrist or their internist for medication evaluation.

The psychiatrist who gets the referral probably schedules ten-minute interviews for these referred patients. For an in-depth psychiatric evaluation (a first interview), I always allotted ninety minutes. There is plenty of evidence that many psychiatrists seeing these referred patients *never* do a thorough evaluation. But they are quick to *try* one of the many psychotropics now available. Prescription written, return in one month! The next visit is likely to be five minutes and in some cases the brief visit is with a nurse practitioner who asks a few questions and renews the medicine.

The sad conclusion from all of this must at times amount to inadequate treatment or even improper treatment. Many patients seeking treatment for a variety of symptoms are not candidates for psychotropics but are persons who need someone to talk to and to help them come to terms with emotionally stressful life events, present and/or past. Listening provides a sanctum for the homeless parts of another.

Research in the psychiatric and neurological sciences increasingly reaches to explain human behavior through microbiology and brain chemistry. That research may provide remarkable insights and valuable medicines to combat well-defined psychiatric disorders. On the other hand, I believe there will always be a large number of people who require *talk therapy* to enable them to recover from serious emotional damage, the result of past or current life events. It is my belief that the working of the human psyche will never be completely reduced to "the right medication."

I did prescribe psychotropics in my practice, but you might note that most, if not all of the patients I've mentioned, were not taking medication. That includes Howard, the angry man, the Cave Junction woman who connected again with her father, the young intelligent girl who was failing in school.

●

When I practiced in Spokane, Washington, there was another patient who was never on medication. This was undoubtedly the most unusual relationship I ever had with a patient. But then Mary was the most unusual patient I ever had. She was a Native American of the Spokane tribe. I always felt Mary was in touch with a spirit world about which I knew very little. Or perhaps I knew some of that world except by other words. There seemed to be a communication between us that never required an exchange of words.

But first, let me tell you how Mary came to be a patient of mine. Her husband appealed to their internist over a situation confronting Mary. The internist referred her to me with the information she was charged with theft and was possibly facing a jail sentence.

Mary came to my office accompanied by her husband. She was a fairly tall woman, probably 5'9". She stood straight and had definite features of her heritage. As I brought her into my office and introduced myself, she made no response. It wasn't timidity or rejection, but more like reserve. I explained her husband's doctor suggested it might be helpful for her to see me. Mary said nothing but continued to look directly at me sitting erect in her chair. I said I was aware of the charge against her and I could possibly be helpful in the matter if she could tell me what had occurred. After another minute or two of silence, Mary continued looking directly at me and began to speak. Her voice was calm and strong. Her words came clearly and without hesitation, but there was no indication they had been prepared or rehearsed.

She had a restaurant in a small village about ten miles outside Spokane. She prepared and served breakfast and lunch five days a week to many workers in the village. Her soup was their favorite dish. One day, as she began her soup preparation, she discovered she was missing a *necessary* spice. She drove to the market where she bought all her groceries. She rushed in, picked up the spice, and when she got to the single open check-out, there was a line. She couldn't spare the time. The men needed the soup by noon. They depended on her. She rushed out of the store thinking she would pay for the spice on her next trip. She was stopped and the police were called. She received notice of a required court appearance.

Mary was a proud and, I'd say, a rather distinguished looking woman. Her spirit clearly belonged with her tribal ancestry and the dignity that once belonged to Native Americans. The thought seemed to come so clearly: "This woman would wither and die in a white man's jail." I wrote a letter to the judge and provided Mary's account of what occurred. I stated I had no doubt of her honesty and of her intention to pay for the spice on her next trip to the store. I also opined that any jail time would be an extremely traumatic and devastating experience for her. I added Mary had agreed to return for additional office visits until the matter was permanently settled. The judge dismissed the case without a hearing, but Mary continued seeing me.

Thus began one of the most remarkable treatment journeys I have ever been on. I continued to see Mary for over three years, until the time I left Spokane. Only one time did she openly display any emotion. But, as hidden as the feelings were, she opened the details of her life to me. This stoic Native American had survived well in a harsh world.

And so the story began! When Mary was about twelve, she, her mother and eight year old brother were walking along the highway between Spokane and Coeur d'Alene, Idaho. A passing car struck and killed her mother and brother. The driver did not stop. Mary's father had left his wife and children several years earlier. Subsequent to the two deaths, Mary was raised by her maternal grandfather who was a stern, strict and somewhat punitive man. He was "the head of the household" and she was little more than a servant girl. But Mary was not to be dominated by "the white man" or by her grandfather.

After finishing high school, she began working in a restaurant at age eighteen. With her natural precocity, she carefully watched all that occurred at the restaurant and came away knowing the restaurant business.

At the age of twenty-one, she married a Caucasian man who left for the Korean War. After the war, he returned, but not to Mary. She had a daughter as a result of their brief marriage encounter. The grandfather captured his granddaughter's affection as she got older. There had been no contact between Mary and her daughter for many years as a result of the grandfather's destructive interference in the relationship. In her forties, Mary married a Caucasian male who appeared about her age. She described him as a kind man who was accepting of all the stray dogs she brought home. Don built a kennel for the dogs while I was seeing her. She was pleased and proud of his work. I believed Don was good to her, but felt they lacked much intimacy or companionship.

Mary had been frugal during her waitressing years, and at some point rented a building in the little town near Spokane. She converted it into a small, but quite successful local restaurant. As the years passed, she continued to save her money and eventually purchased three houses which she converted to rentals. During one of her visits she told me with a slight note of pride she bought an abandoned church in the town and was converting it into a rental property.

Mary would never have used the word "passion," but I would say she had a passion for music. She was a markedly gifted woman. She taught herself to play the violin, the piano, and the saxophone. In spite of her native stoicism, she showed delight when she told me she found an old jukebox and bought it for the restaurant. Sometimes in the evening she would tell her husband she had something to do in the restaurant. She would drive there, pull down the shades, and, with the saxophone, accompany the music on the jukebox. Her tale made me think of primitive, tribal ceremonies. Mary didn't make music just for herself, but also for *a spirit world*. Perhaps I romanticize when I say it seemed she belonged to the clouds, the wild things of the woodlands, the dew drops.

Our relationship was not only rather formal, but it also had its own formalities. When I first saw her my fee was forty dollars per visit. When I realized it was considerably lower than the local psychiatric rates, over a two year period I raised the fee to eighty dollars per visit. From the beginning, Mary always left the forty dollars on a small table near the exit from my consultation room. I never raised her fee and can't really explain why I didn't. Perhaps I felt it would interfere with the formality, the structure, the integrity of our visits. Mary began to leave attractive and expensive books of art or beautiful scenic areas of the world in the outer office and never referred to them. As I recall, I don't think I ever thanked her or mentioned them. It was our formality.

Over a three year period, I saw her at Christmas time, and each year she gave me a beautiful registered Swiss-made music box. I know I thanked her for these. On one occasion she left a beautiful leather bound gilt edged blank-page book with the following note inside:

Always I had planned to fill this book with poetry and music, then hide it carefully away with the saxophone for someone to find years from now and wonder. It isn't going to happen. Your decorator made this room as lovely as a symphony so she can probably fill it with music with no effort. Someone should write in it. Books should not be wasted.

Mary knew nothing about my family, but I still believe she knew my wife decorated my office. How did she know? All I know is she knew, the way all of us *know* things sometimes. Jane cherished the book and now Laura does, but the pages are still empty.

As an ethical position I would normally not take gifts from my patients. Mary was, of course, an exception. I felt it would have been a violation of our relationship had I refused these generous gifts.

During her visits, I occasionally encouraged Mary to talk about her daughter. At some point I suggested she contact her daughter. She was reluctant fearing she might be rejected. I continued to leave the idea open for her to consider. Finally, she acted on it and was pleased with the result. Her daughter came to visit her and brought the grandson Mary had never seen or even knew existed. They continued a caring relationship.

After about a year of regular visits every week or two, Mary said she would call for her next visit. I had an answering service with a live human on the phone. Between patients I would call in and get my messages. On occasion they would tell me someone called but hung up without saying anything. I would call Mary's restaurant and we would make her next appointment. We never talked about the arrangement. She never left a message. It sort of arranged itself; we just carried it out.

The one time Mary exposed deep emotion was the day I told her I would be leaving Spokane. As soon as the words were spoken, Mary made a sound, a sort of controlled shout of pain or anguish. It almost seemed tribal to me, or do I just make too much of it? She was out of the office before I could say another word.

I felt guilty and heartbroken for her—and myself. I waited about two weeks hoping to hear from her. No word! One afternoon I called the restaurant. She answered. I asked her to come back so we could talk at least one more time. She was hesitant and said she wanted to think about it. A few days later, there was a phone call to the answering service and the hang up. I called Mary and we made a "last appointment."

There was a lamp on a small table in the corner of my office. The top was a decorated glass globe with crystals hanging all around. Mary often mentioned how that lamp was a sort of "beacon" in her life when she was worried or feeling sad. During our visit, I gave her the lamp. She was reluctant to accept it, but I persuaded her. I had brought a box and some wrap to keep it safe. I told her we were moving to Baltimore and gave her our address, telling her I would want her to visit our home if she ever came to Baltimore. I never mentioned writing because I thought that would be intrusive. Suggesting a visit was more open and we both knew there was no likelihood she would ever come to Baltimore. It was another of our formalities, I guess. It was but a gesture. She maintained her rather stiff and reserved manner as we said goodbye. She did not offer her hand.

About one year later, there was a letter from Mary's husband. He reported that Mary went out to take care of the dogs one evening. She did not come back inside and when he went out to find her, she was dead. He mentioned there was a lamp that seemed very special to her and he wondered if it may have in some way been connected to me, and if it was, would I like to have it. I replied affirmatively. In the next week or two, the package came in the mail. The lamp was poorly wrapped and was shattered. I let her husband know, as it was evident someone had packed it for him. Within a short time, he sent me a check he received from the insurance. Jane and I used the money to buy a small ornamental tray with two birds on low branches. My lamp given to Mary as a keepsake was returned to me as a memento of Mary. It felt like my gift to her in my going away was returned as her gift to me in her leaving this earth. That was a lengthy report, but to me Mary deserved adequate coverage though I fail in adequate words. She was special.

•

Let me report briefly about a patient for whom medication management was almost our only contact. On her first visit, Virginia told me she was schizophrenic and had been taking Stelazine for several years. It wasn't so much she refused to give me information, she just eluded answering questions. She said enough to convince me she was indeed psychotic. She lived with a man not far out of Spokane. She described her home as being full of manikins dressed in a variety of weird garments. She wanted a six months' supply of medicine and would return to see me in six months. I gave her a refillable prescription to cover six months. She would faithfully call six months later for an appointment to renew the medicine. During one of her visits, she made a random reference to her sleep pattern.

I thought, "Ah, this is my chance to open up something possibly significant and I'll branch off from there." I casually asked, "What kind of dreams do you have?"

She quickly replied, "They're schizophrenic dreams, of course."

Question asked, answer given.

•

While we are in Spokane, let me tell you about one more patient. This one is an example of how we can manage to survive the major events of life, and then because of our diminished emotional reserves suddenly fall apart over something that would otherwise have been relatively insignificant. I was asked to consult on a patient who had just been admitted to the hospital across the street from my office.

After I finished my day, I went to see her. She was and had been mute since admission early that morning. She was admitted because she had taken a knife and cut her neck from one ear to the other. Fortunately, the cut was not deep and had not severed either carotid artery or damaged her larynx. A few stitches and bandaging was all that was required. Her mute state was the crisis of the moment.

When I entered the room I introduced myself and told her I had been asked by her physician to visit her. She said nothing, but avoided eye contact. I sat by the bed and after a few minutes she turned her head so she could see me. I spoke softly and gently encouraging her to consider telling me why she had done what she did. I continued similar comments with silent spaces interspersed.

Finally, her first words: "The water pipe broke."

Then the story unfolded. Her husband had been terminally ill for the past year. She cared for him by herself and rarely left his bedside other than to take care of their needs and maintain household essentials. She did her own shopping and would rush to the store and return as quickly as possible each time fearing he might be dead on her return. The continuing vigil was itself draining for her and coupled with fixing meals, doing laundry, caring for the house, and the mad dashes to the grocery store she was overwhelmed. But she kept going. Her husband died about three months prior to this day's event. She managed his loss with equanimity and had started seeing friends and neighbors who were all supportive toward her.

The morning of this day she was washing dishes in the kitchen sink and suddenly water was running on the floor where she stood. *The water pipe broke.* As the saying goes: "she lost it." Impulsively, unwittingly she grabbed a knife and cut her neck. I saw her again late the next day. Her pastor had been in to see her and several friends had visited. She was going to be discharged the following morning. Her friends planned to take her out to lunch and the pastor had agreed to visit her regularly for a while. I encouraged her to consider grief counseling. No psychotropic was needed. I gave her my card and asked her to call me if she felt a need to talk to me again.

Chapter Thirteen:
Forgive the Unforgiveable: Why?

Most likely the word "unforgiveable" brings to mind memories of incidents that still smolder and quickly surface in your brain. Many people carry an indelible list of grievances from the past. They light up with little or no provocation: a spoken word, a gesture, someone's laugh triggers the memory of an *unforgiveable*. So quickly the memory floods in: the teacher who gave me an unfair grade, the store clerk who was so rude, the doctor who forgot my name, the pharmacist who gave me someone else's prescription, the friend who didn't even smile at my best joke.

Some of us carry short lists, maybe five or ten people and their "offensive behaviors." Others may have lists with ten or twenty miscreants, some in bright colors that flash when the offender comes to mind. There are just no excuses for their behavior. You and I would never behave that way. Well, we may have made a mistake on occasion but when we recognized it we were quick to apologize. No need to carry a list of the few mistakes we made. Anyway they were never serious and we certainly didn't mean to offend anyone.

Just thinking about "those people" brings anger and upsets our day. I quit going to that store ten years ago, but that nasty clerk is still in my head. They don't get *my business* anymore. Someone told me her husband died the week before the incident, but that doesn't give her a right to be rude. And that doctor was good, but being terribly busy was no excuse for forgetting *my* name. My new doctor always remembers my name. The teacher who tried to flunk me died about six months ago. I wish she had taken my memory of her face with her. I guess the pharmacist was just being a fallible human. But someone should report him anyway. Made a mistake once, he'll do it again someday. And the friend who didn't laugh at my joke, well, I got the last laugh. Out of my life!

People should be held accountable for the unforgivable things they do. Of course, if we were all held accountable, there would have to be some exemptions, e.g. if you're a really good person and it was only a little mistake.

We're nice people, and we need to stand up for politeness and what's proper behavior. These offenses can remain with us a long time. My teacher incident was about seventy years ago. No, it was sixty-nine years ago on December 19, 1946. I remember my head was full of Christmas planning when I took that test.

When we think about it calmly and carefully, carrying all these rogues around in our heads is really a burden at times. We never invited them to occupy space in our brain and often wish they would leave. Of course, they don't even know they live in our heads! We create the picture of them we carry around in that little neuron nest we built just for them. It gets overcrowded. It weighs us down. Their presence makes us feel irritable and unfriendly toward everyone.

Let's calmly think this through. How can we rid ourselves of these unwelcome brain-bugs? They do *bug* us. For clarification: forgiveness is really an act of the mind, the intellect, the will. Forgiving is not an emotion; we don't have to *feel* forgiving. All we need to do is just decide: "**I do forgive them**." We'll still *feel angry* as we remember the event (the emotional part), but once our mind can say, "**I forgive**," we'll not remember them as often. Once forgiven, they lose their importance in our minds. Someday we are likely to forget them entirely. And there's a certain inner peace in being a forgiving person. The fabric of society is held together by the threads of forgiveness.

+ + + + + + + + + +

WISDOM

I prayed for wisdom by age ninety-six
The Lord just smiled and answered nix
It leaves me adrift and in rather a fix
To still depend on the same old tricks

The above was a little rhyme I wrote for my 96th birthday, which was about a week ago. I drove the two hundred miles to Demarest, N.J. the day before and spent my birthday with Laura and our two granddaughters, Casey and Tara, ages seventeen and fifteen.

It was a pleasant time as it always is with them. They introduced me to a new game, "Train of Thought." I do enjoy being with them especially when they start laughing and joking with each other. Laura has a grand sense of humor, as did Jane. We went into New York for lunch one day and each of us got a cookie from the famous "Hole in the Wall." People line up in the street and wait their turn to buy a cookie at what is literally a hole in a wall. The trip back was sad for me. I thought of how many times Jane and I made that trip, and how many times Laura brought the girls down to see us during Jane's later Alzheimer's years.

Three days after my return to Vantage House I travelled with Paul and Sharlene from Hagerstown to Bowling Green, KY to see my son John and his family. John's mild stroke ten days earlier was the reason for our visit. Thankfully, there is no residual other an unusual sensation in his left leg. Cause of the event has not yet been determined. At this point, physical changes are minimal but the emotional scar will remain for an indefinite time in his mind as well as in the minds of his wife and three children. I reflected on the blessing of good health all six of my children have.

•

Richard Rohr, O.F.M. has an email site which brings me his spiritual thoughts and guidance each day. He frequently writes about various saints and mystics and their contemplative lives. He touts the importance of contemplation not just in spiritual life but in living.

Within the last week, I wrote down the following quote: "The inner life of quiet, solitude, and contemplation is the only way to find your ground and purpose now." In another place he wrote of the world of mystics "where the light is shining through all the time." I saw an ad recently for *A School of Contemplation.*

I attended a silent week's retreat a few years ago. The retreatants met with the priest-director three times each day. During that time, there were discussions about everyone's spiritual thoughts and needs. Twice each day the director would ask us to sit in silence for twenty to thirty minutes with his recommended posture, breathing rate, and mind "nowhere, empty." He kept telling us to let our mind go to *nowhere*. I asked him one day where "nowhere" is, but he was unable to tell me. The period was the most trying and unpleasant time of the whole week for me.

When the meditation time was over, individuals volunteered to report on their spiritual experience during the time. I remember one man saying during the contemplation time he was walking about in a garden, finding Jesus there and having a lengthy conversation with the Lord. He described the flowers in the garden.

My inner skeptical self could not keep from thinking, "That man just had a hypnagogic experience." Hypnagogic relates to that sort of dream-waking state, often quite vivid, that may occur just before falling asleep or when dozing off in the daytime. Perhaps I was only defending myself for not being able to achieve a similar result. Besides, I have no right to make judgments about another's statements regarding a religious experience. It seems a bit irreverent.

All in all the retreat was a worthwhile experience and had a major impact on my life. It brought light to bear and to clarify some darker times of years past. I came home with the desire, almost a need, to meditate. I've struggled with the desire and the determination to reach that contemplative relationship with God for over two years now. Recently, I've come to believe some people are not capable of mystic-like contemplation and that it is not the only royal road to find the Deity. I've decided my non-meditative state in life does not make me a second-class religious believer. That's a blunt way of making my point, but I have some mild resentment toward those spiritual leaders who seem to minimize those of us who are perhaps unable to or chose not to travel their golden road of prayer. They give the impression contemplative spirituality is *the* way to God.

My parents were as religious and as thoroughly pious as any two people I have ever known. I know my father watched the sky and the clouds and seemed to know a lot about the weather. He also recognized that God determined all the world dad lived in. My mother lived and breathed charity and peace toward everyone she knew and toward the world at large. They prayed *words* as I learned to do and still do. So, I no longer meditate in the mornings. I say prayers I know and use the *Give Us This Day* monthly booklet with daily words of scripture and prayer. Then I usually say some direct and personal things to God about my needs for the day, my gratitude for all the blessings of my life. I just plain speak some of my thoughts to God. Now when I finish my morning prayer I don't go into the rest of my day feeling a bit left out because I failed once more at meditation.

The other bonus of contemplation is said to be "hearing God's voice" in the sacred silence meditation provides. I never achieved that treasured time to hear God speak to me, but I do think God puts ideas in my mind for me to think about, and then leaves me to decide what to do about them. I feel God's grace is often attached to some of my thoughts and I let God know I'm grateful. Summing it up, I think I'll go on praying the way I always have.

I believe I mentioned in the beginning of this book I don't like talking on the phone, primarily because I can't see the person I'm talking to. I suspect if indeed I were to hear God's voice, then I would want to see God. I've thought sometimes I would like to hear Jane speak to me, but I would then so desperately need to see her. I'm content to wait for the afterlife to have that level of contact with the Deity and with Jane. (I write as if I had a choice about it).

If I may speak from a psychological point of view, I wonder if some brains are better equipped or perhaps better connected so meditation is easier for them. Let me change that from "better" to differently equipped or connected. The Lord said, "…unless you become as little children." There's my answer, I pray like children pray!

I wonder if contemplative people fall asleep more easily. They have the ability to empty their minds, and *off to la-la land*. I fall asleep by concentrating. I have developed an alphabetic list of saints whom I ask to pray for me as I fall asleep. During some of my repetitious weight exercises in the mornings, I pray to saints in the same way and go through approximately eighty names during that time. That leaves me starting with the J's at bedtime. I rarely get through the M's before I'm asleep. As age would have it, I get up two or three times during the night and can usually pick up the names where I left off. On the worst nights I may get to the S's or T's.

Distraction is really the difficulty in the prayer life of most people. It's difficult enough to concentrate when I have words to cling to, but for me to even try to float off into an empty mind only leaves an open field for random thoughts. Some spiritual directors speak of *consciousness* as opposed to *conscience*. I do find an increasing desire and ability to be conscious of God's presence in life, in other people, in nature, in the moment, and in the *now and this*.

Before leaving the topic, I will mention in addition to their goodwill, genuine spirituality, and generosity of spirit those who publicize the need for a strong contemplative element in our prayer life often have some financial gain from their giftedness. That is certainly their due. But I'm uncomfortable sometimes when I sense a note of superiority in the way they speak of their "contemplative life and experiences."

•

When we lived in Spokane we attended Lenten lectures at a Jesuit parish. I still remember the simplicity and elegance of Father Nigro's lectures. He's the first priest I ever heard say he believed if a young couple, honestly intending to get married, lived together with "sexual benefits" (as the young people say) they were not living in sin. And this was in the early eighties. He foreshadowed Margaret Farley's book *Just Love: A Framework for Christian Sexual Ethics*. Farley's book is a remarkably erudite, well documented commentary on current sexual mores. The book was more than frowned upon by the Catholic Bishops Conference.

Another memorable item from Father Nigro's lectures was his suggestion we invite Jesus to visit us, and just sit and chat with the Lord as we would with a friend. He suggested we could call God by any name that was comfortable for each of us. Since Jane died, I increasingly find myself talking to her about things that happen, where I'm going, what I'm doing or planning to do. I also increasingly talk to God, also out loud when in my apartment. Then I end up using the wrong name sometimes, e.g. asking God to help me find something when I meant to address the request to Jane. I've thought I might solve the problem by addressing the Lord by the name Jane. This might get a bigger and quicker response—sort of double or nothing.

•

I had occasion to ask for help recently. It was a major "senior moment" from which I gratefully recovered. The Sunday before I went to Laura's for my birthday, I looked in my file cabinet to take some cash I was keeping there. It was gone, over $300. I couldn't believe it. I checked through all the files in the drawer and found our passports and two store credit cards were also missing. I went down immediately and reported it to security. The manager on duty and the security person both came to my apartment. They searched the file drawer and the one under it. They asked if I might have moved it to some other place. I was positive I hadn't. I said I might have moved the money, but I would not have moved the passports or the credit cards.

The Plant Operations Manager, the Administrator of Vantage House, and the Director of Social Work Services all paid me a visit or two after I returned from the visit to Laura's. The Executive Director of Vantage House also called me. They all, in one way or another, brought up the key question: had I possibly moved the items and forgotten? Of course, I hadn't done so and I would remember if I had, plus the fact I would never have put them together. I even framed a story in my mind so I thought I knew when they were taken, how it happened and who my suspect was. I told Laura the sad story and then repeated it when I saw Paul and Sharlene. I decided never to mention the theft to any of the other residents and thankfully I did not.

You, my kind reader, know the rest of the story and will surely have a sympathetic ear because the same thing has probably happened to you or to one you love. One night at dinner, for no particular reason, I began to wonder if I might have moved the items. I slept rather fitfully. The next morning I checked every closet, shelf, and cubbyhole. After two hours of looking and almost ready to give up, I looked in the three drawer chest in the bathroom. In the last drawer I opened I found the missing items in a folder. I apologized to each individual involved and must say everyone was extremely gracious with a comment about their own similar experiences.

The moral for me has been to recognize how bull-headed I can be and have been at times. I hope neither Jane nor any of my children have suffered too much from that stubborn streak I have to live with.

•

Let me leave that uncomfortable item behind and bring up something with a bit of levity. I consulted at the National Security Agency from 1962 until I left the area in late 1966. I was given a metal admission badge with my picture and a number on it. There was an attached metal chain to put around my neck. I consulted one or two mornings each week and in the afternoon I returned to my office.

During an afternoon subsequent to my being at NSA, I was seeing a patient whom I had been seeing for several weeks. As we talked, I realized the badge and chain were in my suit coat pocket. I wanted to transfer them quietly to my desk drawer and not disturb our interaction. I thought I made the transfer without the patient noticing. That evening after dinner I had a call from the patient.

"Dr. McAllister, I just had to tell you how wonderful the session was today and how helpful you were."

I thanked her for the comment, but felt I needed to gain a better sense of this almost miraculous technique I had apparently developed.

So I asked, "What was it you found so helpful today?"

Her reply: "When you took your rosary beads out of your pocket to pray for me, I was so grateful and knew I would get better."

I do have considerable respect for the power of suggestion as well as for the rosary. My recollection is that the patient continued to improve gradually as I anticipated she would.

The patient called me because she was given my home number when she became my patient. All my patients were given my home number with the comment, "If you NEED to get in touch with me, here's my home number. You may call me anytime if it's necessary." I rarely had calls that were not appropriate. Remember, this was all before the cell phone age.

•

We had a speaker here the other day from the Johns Hopkins Applied Physics Laboratory. Of course, he talked about space exploration and the space rocket that passed by Pluto on July 14 of this year. I was unable to attend the lecture and probably wouldn't have understood enough about the subject to fully appreciate it.

His topic did remind me of a patient in his late teens whom I saw many years ago. He was a bright young man, but was not being successful in his first year of college. His mind seemed to wander to subjects other than those covered in his classes. One day he was speculating about space exploration and how far humans might travel someday.

Probably to encourage him in his discourse I asked, "What do you think is on the edge of space?"

His immediate and rather unperturbed matter-of-fact reply was, "Sagebrush."

It seemed such a clever nonchalant comment. But the question remains in my mind.

With the news about Pluto, I've started wondering again, "What is on the edge of space? How does space end, stop, or shut down?" Perhaps it doesn't! Our finite minds put everything in a time and space context. Since Jane is now in that state of eternal existence, I sometimes ask her, "What is it like where there is no *time*, no day, no night?" Eternity is unfathomable. Perhaps the same is true of space even though inconceivable. How can distance be interminable? But how can time be unending? We assume everything must end. Or might it just change? Or just *be?*

•

A topic close to the above comes to mind. Thomas Aquinas, the great Dominican theologian and philosopher of the 13th century, was the centerpiece of my philosophy studies in college. Aquinas taught that all things that exist have two fundamental principles: existence and essence. Essence is "what a thing is." Existence is "that a thing is." Or one might say *existence* actualizes the potency of *essence*. *Existence* provides quiddity. Next we have *substance* and *accidents*. A natural thing has substance and exists in its own right. Accidents are modifications substances undergo, but do not change the kind of the substance nor do they exist in their own right.

My essence is animal; my substance is human; my accidents include my sex, color of my skin, etc. By now you must be questioning: "Why is he writing all this? Is he just showing off a bit of philosophy he once studied?" We are now where I've been going.

In both the Old Testament and the New Testament, God says; "I am, Who am." To me that sounds like *God is existence*. When someone asks me who I am, my response is "I am Robert McAllister." The *"I am"* and the *"Mc"* are both significant. *Mc* indicates I'm the son of Allister (as of long ago somewhere). *I am* indicates I am of God, of *Who Am*.

So, my conclusion to all of this is whatever exists anywhere exists because it is of *Whom Am*. God gives quiddity to everything. God not only creates everything; God holds it in existence because God is *am-ness*. I do not see this as pantheism by any stretch of the imagination, although it does indicate to me God is part of all that is. The thought also gives me a new respect for the squirrels, the birds, even the ants, in fact all living things. *Who Am* is involved in all things that exist.

No wonder Pope Francis has recently said, "God will judge you on how you cared for the earth." No wonder we pray, "God, hold me in the palm of Your Hand."

•

As I sit here rereading what I just wrote, the thought comes to me, "I've known this all my life, not as clearly, not as certainly as I do now, but it has been there." And I wonder how I knew it. The answer is my childhood on the ranch, the world of nature. As my father knew, I knew God controlled the weather. It wasn't so much God controlled the weather; it was *God's wind, God's rain*, and *snow*, and *sun*. They were *God's stars* that filled the sky, that made the milky-way traverse the heavens like broad contrails, and that made Northern Lights dance in colorful shapes through the night. It was *God's grass* that grew and fed the livestock in the summer months, and *God's hay* we gathered and stored to feed the cattle and horses in the cold, snow-covered fields of winter. It was *God's water* that came from the snow-capped mountains through miles of aquifers and then bubbled out of the ground in an endless flow.

•

This afternoon I walked through God's trees and stood at my little sanctuary on the bridge overlooking God's man-made Lake Kittamaqundi. There was a slight breeze that moved the leaves. I watched and saw each leaf perform its own special dance. All were of the same substance, but each had its own accidents. Those accidents of Thomas Aquinas are what make each leaf respond differently to the breeze and make each snowflake of winter special. The *accidents* of individuals cause them to respond to the breath of life as the leaves respond to the wind. Our *Aquinas accidents* influence and often direct the way we respond to life's adventures.

•

I have always thought farmers and sailors are more religious than other people. Perhaps they are more likely to pray because they are so closely connected to God's world of nature. That doesn't necessarily mean they are churchgoers or espouse any religion. (After crossing the Atlantic fifteen days on a troop ship, I can understand a sailor's prayerfulness).

Life on the ranch also gave me firsthand acquaintance with life, death, and suffering. Most young people these days may become remotely aware that grass, and trees and flowers live and die. They may become acquainted with death when a relative dies and with new life when someone has a baby. Having pets may also bring them contact with these realities. But for the most part, their experience is limited by the city-suburb culture in which most of us live.

My youth was replete with experiences of life beginning and of its ending. The just-out-of-the-shell chicks that were not doing well were kept and nurtured in the house behind the kitchen stove until they were stronger. The newborn calf, too weak to suckle, was bottle fed until it could stand and find the cow's teat. The pregnant heifer waiting its first birth was watched through the night by someone sleeping in the barn to be there to aid in the delivery if necessary. Rancher turned veterinarian often helped the delivery with a strong and vital pull of an extended leg. The dog, inexperienced with porcupines, had quills carefully and gently removed following its first lesson. The faithful saddle horse nearing the end of life was mercifully shot for relief of pain.

Then how should I understand the reality that came when some of these living creatures were sacrificed for our own needs? How can I explain the impact made on my thinking, my caring and my concern for their life and wellbeing? We believed all life is sacred. It was our faith. It was our practice. Save the chick. Save the newborn calf or colt or piglet. Were we just being selfish, saving them so we could eat them or sell them later? That was not the motivation for their care. They were saved because they had life and life should be preserved; and their untimely death was not acceptable to those who were responsible for their immediate care.

We raised wheat and oats, we raised cattle and pigs and chickens to feed the world. God's bountiful provision for God's flock included us. The time came when our needs were put ahead of the needs of the animals we cared for and nourished. Dad would cut the heads off a couple of roosters so we could eat them for Sunday dinner. My mother feathered them and cleaned out the entrails. We would kill and butcher a pig. Dad would kill him by hitting him in the head with a sledge hammer, and then cut his throat to bleed him properly. When we butchered a steer Dad would shoot him in the head. The animal to be butchered was hung by the feet from a beam and then the bloody work took place. When we hunted and killed deer they were field-dressed and then the remains brought home. When we shot prairie chickens or pheasants they were given to Mom to feather and clean. This all seems rather gruesome and heartless as I write about it, but not so when I consider how it was then. It was the reality of life on the ranch and came as a natural part of that world. Killing deer and wild birds was not just for sport. They supplemented our meat supply.

•

Of course, I also participated in the painful severity of branding calves in the early summer. The cows and calves were driven into one big corral. One by one we roped each calf and dragged it to the branding fire where a heated iron burned our brand on the right flank. As the calf's mother came close to protect her young, the mother was shooed out of the corral. By the end of the branding, the calves were all separated from their mothers. It was weaning time. The calves would now live on grass, hay, and grain as needed. And the cows would bellow mournfully for days to come. After two or three weeks the calves would rejoin their mothers, but by then the calves no longer looked for nursing mothers and the cows' milk was no longer available.

Both my parents were gentle, kind, and tender-hearted persons. They also faced life as pioneers and knew the hardships of the world they chose. How far I've come from those beginnings! But the life I shared with them remains with me now and gives me feelings of compassion for the harshness in others' lives and gratitude for the blessings in my own.

When I read the scriptures or hear sermons about the Good Shepherd, I often wish cattle had been the important livestock of the times. Cowboys would then be the example of the caring, tender herder knowing each of his herd by name. Dad was a model caretaker of his flock. The cattle and the horses were fed and taken care of before the ranch hands. And if ever one strayed and got lost, we would search until it was found.

•

I just returned from the grocery store. So many times during the day when I do something as seemingly insignificant as that, I am filled with gratitude to God. I am so blessed that at age ninety-six I can drive to the store, shop for the groceries I need to prepare my breakfast and lunch every day, and return home and carry them to my apartment. It brings one of those "now and this" prayers of gratitude. These happen often in my typical day and it's not unusual for the gratitude to spread back to the gift of my parents, my friends, Jane and the life and love and faith we shared for fifty years. The gratitude easily spreads back in time to the land where I grew up, to the road I've travelled and to the people I met along the way. I don't just remember these events, these people. They live in my mind, in my heart and each day they fill *My Cup of Life* which overflows with tears of gratitude.

Chapter Fourteen:
Boxed In

Perhaps you can still remember the number of boxes you had when you moved to Vantage House. I mention this to introduce a delicate subject I'm going to write about. I hope you do not find it inappropriate or offensive. I have considered writing it for some time, so it is not done on sudden impulse or in response to any particular event.

You wonder: what could be offensive about boxes? It is not the box that offends. It is the reality in the box, a reality that many of us avoid thinking about and prefer not to hear mentioned. There are some inescapable realities of life that are difficult to confront directly, although they float around in the same brain that plans your next shopping trip or whom you will have dinner with tonight. The latter events require clear thinking, some preparation. You make a list for the shopping trip and decide where you want to shop. You call people to make arrangements for dinner, the time, the day, maybe what you will wear.

Perchance we crowd our minds with a milieu of daily life decisions in order to quiet the silently harbored question: And after this what? And after that? And after? And? No matter how many boxes brought you to Vantage House, there will only be one when you leave. You may find that a harsh, even brash statement. It is confrontational. It is perhaps haunting, but it is real.

If you have stayed with me this far, you may wonder why I dared raise the question. Like the shopping trip or the dinner plans, this too should involve some preparations. I'm not talking about legal issues, your estate, your belongings, and those precious items you hold so dear. I'm talking about you, the living container of your thoughts, your attitude, your spirit, your dreams, your hopes, your fears.

This is a time to remember the good things you have done for others during your lifetime: helping a classmate years ago, resolving a quarrel friends were having, helping neighbors with a house or yard problem, calming someone who was troubled, the kindnesses that dotted your relationships with others, the generosity of your smile, a positive exchange with a stranger. Perhaps you spoke in defense of someone who was being intimidated or someone who was the victim of another's bias or outright bigotry. Search your memories for the sunshine you brought to one who was sad, the balm you applied to one who was hurting, the boost you gave to one who was discouraged.

This is also a time to remember the good others brought into your life, the kindness and care not just of those especially dear, but of countless others as well. Search through the wealth of your past experiences and find the jewels of gentleness that sometimes came so unexpectedly, the tender word of a stranger when you were sad, the friend who sat with you during a difficult time, those who kept in touch through the years because they cared about you. Recall the treasure of someone's ready smile, the cookies some special person made, the greeting at work that always brightened your day, the one who thought to call you when your life seemed to be in shambles.

It might be worth your time to give some thought to the negative, the sometimes hostile things you have done or planned to do. Was there a demeaning attitude toward a neighbor, participation in harassment of a classmate or coworker, negative attitudes and comments about someone of a different race or religion or sexual orientation? Were you caustic and critical toward someone who didn't meet your standards? If in your review of these areas of life you find yourself a bit lacking, it might improve your peace of mind to regret the behavior which was less than your true standards would require. Being sorry for something that was harsh, unkind, or inappropriate can be a healing experience.

You may have a little box in your mind where you store the hurtful things others have done: the friend in school who betrayed your trust, the co-worker who was consistently rude, the relative who was unkind and sometimes cruel, the noisy or perhaps nosey difficult neighbor, or negligence of one close to you. Harboring hurts from the past muddies our life, clutters our mind, and darkens our perspective.

This is a time for healing wounds which only drain life's resources, wounds better not left to fester in oneself or in others if possible. Forgiving oneself and others occurs within the mind and heart. Reconciliation perhaps? It's time!

+ + + + + + + + +

Dreams apparently have held considerable interest throughout the history of most cultures. There are hieroglyphics in Egypt depicting dreams and their interpretations. Sigmund Freud was prominent in bringing dream interpretation to the field of psychology and psychiatry. He believed wish fulfillment was the motivation for all dreams. Carl Jung had a broader point of view with the position that dreams reflected the entire personal and collective unconscious.

In therapy, I never focused on patients' dreams specifically, but in reviewing their sleep history I would reference their dreams. I did not discuss the dreams at length unless I thought they had definite pertinence. For the most part, I have given little attention to my own dreams. I have noticed, since Jane's death, I am almost always alone in my dreams. I am not only alone, but I am often lost either in a strange city or a strange building. There are many people around, but no one seems aware of my presence and there's no one whom I would approach for help. At times, I dream of doing work with my brother Don. We are usually working on some sort of building, and the job is not going well.

These dreams are not really frightening but there is a strong sense of helplessness in the "lost dreams" and a sense of frustration in the "work dreams." Certainly these dreams reflect my current situation. I fear getting lost and I don't drive to unfamiliar areas. When I'm alone I only go to stores I am familiar with or I went to in the past with Jane. Getting through the day sometimes seems like work and there are days when the things I do are somewhat frustrating.

I had two recurring dreams many years ago which, in retrospect, clearly related to my life at the time. In one of the dreams, I was in a field and completely surrounded by fire which continued to burn closer until I woke briefly. During the same period of time, I had a recurring dream of riding in the back of a car with a woman I had never seen before and whom I seemed to idolize. I believe both dreams related to my marital situation, my sense of helplessness, and increasing loss of meaning in my marriage to Marguerite, and my desire for a partner who would be a close companion. Neither dream recurred after I met Jane. (And the car took us across the country to Reno).

Rather than seeing dreams as an expression of the unconscious mind, I always saw them as an expression of current emotional conflicts that were quite identifiable. I found that to be true in my own dreams and in patients' dreams on those occasions when we discussed their dreams.

•

Until now, I have failed to make any reference to an extremely important friend in my life, one who has been influential both in my spiritual world and my temporal world. He is one of those friends who are *always there* even when I haven't seen him in months or heard from him in weeks. I met Joe in 1985, the first year I began teaching in the Pastoral Counseling Program at Loyola in Baltimore.

Joe was a priest of the Philadelphia Archdiocese, but had joined Maryknoll, a community of missionaries, when the opportunity occurred. He had returned from the missions in Venezuela to take the program at Loyola. Jane and I joined a few of the students and their friends at a get-together about every month. It seemed like we and Joe were *simpatico* from the very beginning and our friendship with him developed.

Joe completed the program and returned to his work in Venezuela. Then one day, he got in touch with me and asked if I would come to Venezuela as a consultant for his work. I replied I would not come unless I could bring my secretary, meaning Jane of course. He was pleased and arrangements were made. It was a life-changing experience.

Over the years, Jane and I travelled to Venezuela three times to work with Joe. On the first trip, we stayed at the Maryknoll house in Caracas. Joe was always a wonderful host and showed us *the sights* in the area. On that trip, he took us up to the barrios in the hills outside Caracas. Access to the area required a jeep-like vehicle or walking. The latter was of course the common way of getting through the squalid areas to the higher regions, equally steeped in poverty. We visited two lay missionaries who lived there and worked with the poor in the area. Jane and I had never witnessed such abject poverty. It left us with an indelible memory of the needs of the poor and inspired us to respond prayerfully and financially to such needs.

My work seemed to be talking to Joe about his work, helping him expand his thinking, and discussing at length particular problems. He did ask me to meet with the bishop in the area regarding a specific matter. Caracas was, as so many cities, a sharp contrast between wealth and poverty. There was a spectacular outdoor theater where we attended an opera.

•

As an aside, about twelve years ago Jane and I became friends with a couple from Venezuela who live in the Baltimore area. We met at an art show where various venders were selling their wares. Maria sold beautiful ceramic pieces which she made. After seeing her and her husband several times, we invited them for lunch and later visited their home. To our surprise, we learned that her husband, Ricardo, was a good friend of Hugo Chavez. He showed us a picture of Chavez holding Ricardo's grandchild.

This couple explained that the people of Caracas didn't like Chavez because he built cable-trams to the mountain barrios. The barrio people were grateful because they did not have to walk down to the city to work and then walk back up at the end of the day. But the people of the city were angry at Chavez because the barrio people could now come down to visit the city on weekends and holidays. The city people didn't want them there except as a work force. All of this is probably not unlike many American cities. Keep the poor in *their own area* after the work is done.

•

The second time we visited Joe in Venezuela was in Barinas where we stayed with him in the barrio. His house was a living room, one bedroom, a bath, and a kitchen-dining area without a roof. We had the bedroom and Joe slept in a hammock in the living room. It was an unusual experience to pick fruit from a tree which had branches hanging over his kitchen.

Joe had started a breakfast program for the young school children. He supplied the food and the mothers would take turns preparing it in their homes. The children would come to that house in the morning and have something to eat before going to school. Jane and I contributed to that program as long as I had my psychiatric practice.

Our third visit was also in Barinas. Joe was living with another Maryknoll priest and we stayed with them in their apartment. During this visit, Joe took us on a fascinating trip in his jeep over the Andes Mountains to Merida. We stayed overnight in that beautiful resort city of Venezuela. I found it remarkable the hotel where we stayed had windows in the rooms, but without glass or screens. Apparently, the temperature was moderate year round and the air was free of mosquitoes and flying bugs.

With some local assistance and donors from the U.S., Joe developed a clinic for the poor. It was really like a small local hospital. We were there when a team of doctors from Operation Smile International visited and performed surgical procedures. Primarily, they operated on children with major oral malformations. It was quite an experience to see these doctors in this foreign country doing work which was paid for by donors in the United States.

During that visit, Joe and I talked at length about his plan to select a small group of people and train them to be counselors. I joined him in the first meeting of the group and participated with the benefit of Joe's translating. His idea was to train them to work with the simple problems that typically develop in families or in local social situations. That program was still in existence just a few years ago when Joe last visited Venezuela.

Joe returned to the U.S. a few years after our last visit. He is retired now after 35 years in the missions of Venezuela. Currently, he is helping in a Spanish-speaking parish outside of Philadelphia. He has written two books on English and Spanish idioms and has recently published *What They Taught Us*.

We are intermittently in touch, but overshadowing that is the knowledge we each have a dear friend with whom we are united in prayer and goodwill.

●

Since I've written about an important friend, the thought comes to me to write about my "shepherds of St. John's" as I privately refer to them in my thoughts and prayers. Jane and I joined the St. John the Evangelist congregation in Columbia, MD, about twenty years ago. We were active on one of the committees for several years. As most churchgoers seem to do, we began going to the same service each Sunday, the 9 a.m. Mass. And as most churchgoers seem to do, we picked the same seats every Sunday. Now one of my closest friends is the woman who always sat next to Jane.

Over the years strong friendships formed and finally sorted themselves out to two or three couples and two or three individuals who are now lifelong friends. It seems strange to use that particular word *lifelong* as if they have always been present in our lives. In a way, perhaps they have been. They are prototypes of those with whom we formed friendships in the past. While we may not have similar interests, we have comparable beliefs and values, and we resonate with each other emotionally. Perhaps what we share most deeply is a sense of compassion for others and our common spirituality.

These friends from the 9 a.m. Mass are in truth my shepherds since Jane died. I know each one is genuinely concerned for my welfare and would be available for any help I might need. I look forward to seeing them every Sunday, and getting a hug from five or six women on a Sunday morning makes a great beginning for my week. Being with one or two of them socially is always gratifying and ever special. The love they had for Jane is important in our relationship. As I write that, the thought comes to me: I feel more comfortable with people who knew Jane, whether or not reference to Jane enters in our conversation. Comments relating to Jane would be welcome and understood if made. There are a decreasing number of residents here at Vantage House who knew Jane or remember her. In a subtle, but very distinct way, there is always a barrier for me in any relationship I have where Jane is unknown.

•

Back in 1991, I wrote an article titled *Mother Church, Doctor Freud* which was published in *Sisters Today*, September 1991, Volume 63, Number 5. I would like to quote the beginning paragraphs of that article because I believe the position taken is still pertinent. I quote:

"A review of the relationship between the Catholic Church and the mental health professions over the past five decades reveals patterns of interaction that raise questions about the present soundness of their association. Initial exchanges between Mother Church and Doctor Freud were fraught with suspicion and outright hostility. A period of reconciliation followed, but more recently the chasm between the two appears to be widening. . ."

"There is considerable evidence Mother Church still has grave doubts about Doctor Freud. As a direct result of her continuing doubts, which are based on a history of early suspicion and a current lack of impartial information, Mother Church has during the past three decades fostered the development of a hybrid psychiatry detached from mainstream psychiatry, but considered acceptable to church administrators. In turn, this hybrid psychiatry provides to church administrators the kind of information which supports its own existence. The circle closes, and the system becomes insulated. Church-affiliated mental health care, i.e., mental health treatment that is church-supported, church-organized, or in any way church-controlled, does not provide disinterested, dispassionate, independent treatment of women and men religious; nor does it provide unbiased and impartial information to administrators of religious. In the creation of a hybrid system of care, the Church perpetuates its mistrust of mainstream psychiatry and deprives church personnel access to the extensive system of care the mainstream mental health professions offer. . ."

"When Catholic religious require inpatient treatment, they are often sent to institutions that provide church-sponsored and therefore church-approved treatment, presumably 'safe' institutions. Should each religion have its own mental health professionals, its own mental hospitals to treat its own ministers? Or is it only Catholic religious who require such unusual care. . ."

"This is the age of managed care, including psychiatric care. Managed care refers to the fact the third-party payers demand proof of need for treatment, both inpatient and outpatient. There is no blank check, no open-ended program for anyone receiving mental health treatment, except for Catholic religious who seek treatment in the church-affiliated system. . ."

•

I was President of the National Guild of Catholic Psychiatrists at the time this article was written. At the end of the year of my presidency, I recommended the Guild be discontinued because the reasons for its existence were no longer present. Psychiatry was more broadly accepted in society as a whole. As a result, Catholics approached psychiatric care more easily and more willingly when a need arose. The National Guild voted to end its existence that year.

It was also my thought psychiatrists generally had become more adept at working with people of faith. Now I wonder if that is true considering some of the present changes in psychiatric care. My approach to all patients included asking them if they belonged to any faith group and the second important question was: "Are you practicing your religion?" If a patient was a practicing member of a religion, I was alerted to inquire from time to time what their religion might believe or recommend in a certain situation. I wanted to expose and differentiate any guilt feelings they might have because of their religious beliefs. If that were the case, those guilt feelings would be dealt with more delicately and in relation to their beliefs. I believe this position should be a standard of care for all therapists. However, I fear the area may be increasingly neglected in the short session time of most current psychiatric care.

I was also the director of the Isaac Taylor Institute of Psychiatry and Religion when I wrote the article quoted above. The facilities under Catholic Church auspices were therefore competitors in the field. Religion professionals in the Isaac Taylor Institute were not all Catholic and their treatment program, except for one group meeting each week, was conducted in conjunction with all adult patients in the same facility.

•

Let me give an example of the unjust and autocratic "care" that can occur in a church supported psychiatric facility. In my late years of practice, a priest (we'll call him Fr. Jim) was referred to me by a therapist whom I knew well. The priest had been sent to a church facility because his superior thought he might be a pedophile. The superior's decision was based on finding the priest had some internet pictures of young children playing on the beach naked. He was referred to Institution *Nameless*. After three days of evaluation, Jim was sent back to his community with the recommendation that he return for long term care "sooner rather than later."

He returned to Nameless in a matter of days. He was there for eight months, and during that time his records referred to him as a pedophile, although he consistently denied he was a pedophile or that he had ever engaged in such behavior. His community would not accept him back without a recommendation from the facility stating he was ready to return. The facility would not give him that recommendation until he admitted he was a pedophile. Finally, in desperation and in order to get out of his "imprisonment" he said he was a pedophile. Essentially, that was the end of his functioning as a priest.

He returned to his community. He was to attend three sexual addicts meetings each week, to have individual and group counseling once a week, and to return to Nameless every six months for two years, and then once a year for two more years. Jim requested a second opinion. He was sent to another church supported facility for Catholic religious. Records from Nameless were of course provided. And as one might expect he came back with essentially the same diagnosis, "pedophilia by history in remission." Who would dare contradict the prior diagnosis made by a respected Catholic supported facility? Who would run the risk of putting even a *possible pedophile* back in society?

Jim's referring therapist as well as Jim's confessor did not believe he was a pedophile. After an evaluation and continued interviews over a short period of time, I thoroughly agreed with their conclusion. The three of us appealed to his major superior and he magnanimously agreed to have another evaluation done at the National Institute for the Study, Prevention and Treatment of Sexual Trauma at the Johns Hopkins University School of Medicine. That facility has been designated as a National Resource Site by the United States Department of Justice.

Their conclusion: "However, based on the evidence made available to us, there is nothing to suggest the patient, who has never in the past acted in a sexually improper manner with a child, would do so in the future." They had, of course, reviewed the records from the two prior hospitalizations.

Their report was of no avail. Jim has never been able to say Mass publicly or serve the public in any manner. The Archbishop circumvented the blame by saying he consulted the diocesan attorneys who recommended he not "take the chance." That is the story of psychiatric practice and care under the indirect supervision of the Catholic Church. It is an inadequate, inane, and cruel response to the sex abuse scandals of the Catholic Church and probably does little to prevent them in the future since even their treatment remains a clandestine affair.

You might wonder about the pictures of little children playing naked on the beach. Jim was serving in a parish which included a Catholic grade school. The children were fond of him and he often took pictures of them on the playground. He collected these. He himself was a rather naïve and relatively immature individual who found the companionship of children pleasant. Pictures of small children playing naked on the beach are hardly provocative. His interest was the children, not their nakedness.

•

Pope Francis will be coming to Philadelphia later this month. It is reported under the leadership of Archbishop Chaput the program will ban Catholic groups supporting LGBT families from having exhibits and workshops. The program has invited anti-gay advocates and those who support "conversion or reparative therapy" to give speeches, lead workshops, and sell books and other materials. This program is billed as "A World Meeting of Families." There are definitely two cultures, two different interpretations of scripture, and two families of faith within the Catholic Church. I will someday know how that duality will be resolved. In fact, by the time it happens I may be in a place to know what will happen even before it does happen.

I can only believe that female or male religious sent to a *Catholic* psychiatric hospital for an alleged sexual disorder of any kind is expected to return to his community or diocese *repaired, converted.* One might wonder what the recidivism rate is among these returnees. An unbiased psychiatric treatment program would work to help each of these people review their early life, search the motives for their vocation, question where they truly would like to be in their life now. And along the way, treatment would help them examine their own questioned behavior, confront and resolve any guilt they may feel, and decide where they can best live out whatever innate sexual issues remain. The goal would be: peace of mind and heart, a future they can be comfortable with, and a life where they can still find God. The goal would not be to meet the needs or expectations of their superior, or to try to live vows they possibly never should have made in the first place.

•

Today is Labor Day. Of course, it brought back loads of memories: the ranch, house repairs and rebuilding, and yards with digging and planting and landscaping. Much of it was hard work and long days. There is not a minute of it I can look back on with disdain or disappointment. Although I might not have valued the moment, I treasure the memories and I appreciate the contribution it made to others. In addition, I firmly believe the work contributed, not only to my physical health, but to the spirit that keeps me going each day. It also contributed to my mind as I learned how to do house repairs and modifications.

When I was working as a psychiatrist, I always had a "project" I was working on in the house or the yard. I wanted, I needed to work with "my hands." I also needed to have the satisfaction of producing something, of seeing a finished project or even a project on the way to being completed. After Jane and I were together, there was double satisfaction because she loved being part of it all, and she was that. She used to enjoy telling the story of our taking out a wall in the Grants Pass house. During the process, I told her it was better if she not go upstairs because the ceiling of the room might fall. I had temporarily removed part of a weight bearing wall.

There was a secondary gain in the house and yard work. Eventually, I could see a finished result and along the way I could see the progress we were making and had made. The benefit of that offset a fundamental difficulty of being a psychotherapist. Progress in psychotherapy is typically a slow and sometimes uncertain process. One sees gain, and then it seems to disappear, only to return in another manner. The terrain is often uncertain, the outcome often unpredictable. Even when treatment is complete, there always remains the capriciousness of human behavior and the fickleness of future events.

But when a cedar-closet is built, it will remain. When a room is painted, the color will not change. When a sink is installed, when an electric line is connected, there will be water and electricity in the room. It will continue to be there. Human behavior even after therapy is not subject to the same certainties.

So, I've come upon the reason I am writing this book. I can't yet hold the book in my hands, but I can see the words on the computer as I read and reread what I have written. Each page is a contribution to what will be, God willing, a finished project. I am not writing to convince anyone of anything in particular. As I said in the beginning, I enjoy, I value the process and before long the project will be complete. There will be another finished project!

Then there will be the question: what do you do now to fulfill this need *to do something*. When I visit Laura I can usually find some yard work to do and that's fulfilling. I expect to have the opportunity to spend some long weekends with Paul and Sharlene helping them with fixing and doing and redoing a number of projects they have on hand. I know I must continue to feel I am being productive. And solitaire doesn't do that.

Chapter Fifteen: Physicians Should Talk to Alzheimer's Patients

After my wife was diagnosed with Alzheimer's, she lived eight years. During that time, we visited twelve physicians: internists and a variety of specialists, including neurologists and psychiatrists.

After appointments, Jane would say, "Why doesn't the doctor talk to me about what's going to happen?" Not one physician ever asked her how she felt about having the disease or what symptoms she was aware of or how her life had changed because of the illness. Not one physician ever said the word "Alzheimer's" to her. Initially, our internist told us she had "dementia." She often referred to that word and her resultant fear she was "going crazy." Do health care professionals think a person has to be a Latin scholar to know that "dementia" means "out of your mind"?

It was heartening to read that *DSM-5* uses the term "neurocognitive disorder" to replace "dementia." Would that the entire medical profession might accept APA's precedent and eliminate "dementia" from their use.

Alzheimer's patients are not out of their minds. They are very much in their minds, and it is a dark, frightening, and lonely place. Perhaps that's why physicians and caregivers don't want to go there. After Jane's death, I asked our internist why he never talked to her about her illness.

His reply: "We believe it will only make the patient depressed and frightened."

What do physicians think is going on in the heads of Alzheimer's patients? Their heads are full of uncertainty, fear, sadness, and a sense of isolation.

I believe most physicians don't talk to their patients about Alzheimer's because in reality they know little about the disease other than it causes memory impairment and periods of emotional instability and limits executive function. Perhaps other physicians feel the press of time during brief appointments. Nevertheless, physicians should talk about it. If they don't know what to say, they should learn.

At age ninety-four, I have been a physician for fifty-seven years. I knew essentially nothing about Alzheimer's and, to my knowledge, had never seen an Alzheimer's patient. As a psychiatrist, I saw patients with "senility" but never Alzheimer's. Or did I just not know what to call it back in the sixties, seventies, eighties, and even the nineties?

Suddenly, I had the sad but love-filled opportunity to be the sole caregiver for my life partner. The experience expanded my knowledge, enlarged my life, strengthened my being, enriched me emotionally, and deepened my faith.

Jane and I talked almost daily, often two or three hours, about what was happening in her head. Her intelligence, emotional depth, uncanny insight, verbal abilities, and trust in me enabled her to share her thoughts and feelings. I was her pupil. She taught me Alzheimer's. I share her insights with others by reporting the last six years of her life in my book *An Alzheimer's Love Story* and in lectures I give on the subject.

Jane described her observations, thought processes, memory, and emotions. Jane might remember only a small segment from an entire episode in our day. For Alzheimer's patients, life is not a running film, but isolated snapshots they try to connect, a jigsaw puzzle with some pieces they will never find. Jane often did not hear sentences, but just words that sometimes never came together with meaning.

Jane's impaired executive function took over and prevented her from completing minor household tasks, even those she enjoyed. She was often "lost" in her immediate environment. Yet, twelve days before her death, we talked calmly and rationally about our plans related to dying and who might die first. Later she thanked me for our talk.

She described her anger, her fears, and her sadness. "It's terrifying to watch my feelings take over and put ideas in my head that I don't want to be there and cause me to say hurtful things I don't want to say," she said. When the storms subsided, she said she felt totally humiliated, scornful of herself, and deeply embarrassed. We spoke openly about these episodes. We called them "Alzheimer's storms" and likened them to summer storms that come and go, last minutes or hours, but always pass. Those lasting for days were blissfully forgotten. At lowest ebb, she wanted to die and threatened suicide. This was her greatest fear in the midst of an Alzheimer's storm: "Someday I will always be like this."

They say, "If you've seen one Alzheimer's patient, you've seen one Alzheimer's patient."

I say, "If you listen long and carefully to one Alzheimer's patient, you will understand all Alzheimer's patients."

+ + + + + + + + + +

The above article was published in *Psychiatric News* June 21, 2013. I have repeated these same ideas in lectures I have given and I generally find the audience in strong agreement.

•

About fifteen months ago, I began to think about the possibility of doing something to benefit some of the Alzheimer's residents here at Vantage House. A resident who had been a good friend of Jane's and mine needed to move to the Assisted Living Unit because of increased memory impairment. She was a neighbor of mine, and after Jane's death we sometimes went to dinner together. She told her family she was reluctant to move because she wouldn't see me anymore. I promised her I would visit her regularly on the Assisted Living Unit. She is one of those I mention below.

For residents in independent living, there is one large dining room where they eat their lunch or dinner. The Assisted Living Unit and the Nursing Unit each have their own small dining room. As a result, most of the residents who are moved to either of the care units, no longer come to the main dining room. They live on two separate floors in another area of the building and rarely have an opportunity to see those who were friends and neighbors before their move. In addition most of them are not allowed to leave their unit unaccompanied either because of their physical condition or because of their cognitive impairment.

As a result of the above, I developed the idea of taking various residents from that unit to the main dining room for dinner. The plan has matured over the past many months and now I have a number of residents in the two care units whom I take to dinner individually five nights a week. Each of them has moderate to severe memory loss. One is completely impaired visually. Several use wheelchairs or walkers. One of the residents from independent living generously and kindly shares her table with us. We will often have another one to three residents from independent living join the table.

It is rewarding to me to watch the pleasure and satisfaction of each guest-resident. They must feel a little like they are back home when they return to the dining room where they ate for so many years and now see again many who were their friends. Without fail, each of them expresses gratitude for the "evening out." It is another *now and this* time for me. Other residents have commented on my kindness in doing this. I'm uncomfortable, embarrassed by the comment. I enjoy doing it and it satisfies a need for me, a need I'm not certain I understand. Most likely it connects me to Jane and the isolation and loneliness she felt even when I was close beside her. My presence could not always bridge the chasm caused by Alzheimer's any more than I bridge the gap for these "guests." The chasm with Jane and the gap with these guests are not bridged, but I hope the space is somehow brighter and less frightening.

There is a great variation among those I bring to dinner. One is rather sullen and mildly irritated over any mention of memory impairment. Another is confused by the memory loss and says she is stupid or maybe going crazy.

My response is, as it was to Jane, "You are not stupid and you are not going crazy. Your memory is not functioning as it used to. It is wearing out. And that is happening to all of us as we get older."

Another sometimes jokes about her memory loss. As she left an activity one evening to come with me, I asked what the activity was about. Her playful response:

"That was two seconds ago, do you expect me to remember."

She is a charming woman and engages in a bit of humor quite often. Several of them say in one way or another, "My memory is gone. But I am fortunate to be here and I still enjoy what I do." I don't ask the person what he or she does, because they wouldn't know.

The kind woman who shares her table with us hears the same stories each time one of the guests returns. They cling to pieces of the past that still remain, and tend to repeat them each time we are together. For most, there are very few pieces still available. The occasional visits with their family members rarely provide much enhancement of past events.

One of my dinner guests on occasion mentioned what were probably rather vivid hallucinations. He told me he would be leaving to go back to work. If I asked him where he would be working, his response

"I'm not allowed to talk about that."

As with many of our residents, he must have worked for a secret government project or agency. I felt fairly certain he had Frontotemporal Cognitive Impairment rather than Alzheimer's. Another of my guests appears to have advanced Parkinson's disease. I might mention there are about ten different causes of cognitive impairment. Alzheimer's is the most common cause. Over all the months I've been doing this, there have been at least four of my guests who have died. When it happens I feel like I've lost a friend. And I hope I have been a friend to each of them.

•

Laura's older daughter, Casey, will be going to college next year. She was asked by her College Advisor to write three essays to include with her application. One of these essays follows (with Casey's permission).

Memories
by Casey McConville

Rooting through my dresser, haphazardly flinging clothes into the "give-away" pile, I almost overlooked the silk robe stuffed tightly into the corner of the bottom drawer. I didn't remember leaving it there. My memory of its existence had begun to slowly fade in harmony with memories of Gram herself. The robe had been hers. I had picked it out from her belongings after she died three years ago. Its powdery pink hue and delicate floral design had seemed like the perfect embodiment of Gram's girly elegance. Reaching into my drawer, I carefully unearthed it from beneath a heap of clothes, simultaneously unearthing a flood of memories as I pulled it towards me. I pressed my face into the fabric and inhaled sharply, anticipating the indescribably grand perfume that lingered in the folds. That's just how she would've described it: grand.

To Gram, everything had been grand, from buttons to doilies to windows. She had held an uncanny fascination with life's small wonders. Little treasures had not only captivated Gram, they had obsessed her. She would refuse to leave restaurants without stuffing a stack of napkins from the dispenser into her bag. She would save the used wrapping paper after we opened our gifts on Christmas morning. Her various collections could be found all over her apartment—piles of notebooks in every shape and size; drawers full of hair curlers; tree branches that had been too beautiful to leave sitting outside. Gram would fixate on an object, and from that moment on, it had to be hers. There was simply no dissuading her.

A part of Gram had always been this way, but the quality had not always been so severe. At a certain point in Gram's life, simple fascinations had begun to morph into serious obsessions and eventually dire needs. If she couldn't have something, she would yell at my grandfather, or sneak it into her purse, or throw a tantrum. My grandfather called these moments her "storms". I bore witness to many of the moments, but they never became any easier to watch or understand. Part of me would hate Gram for causing a scene and for acting like a child. But then I would remind myself again and again that it wasn't her fault. In these moments of rage, I was no longer watching Gram; instead, I was watching a cruel manifestation of the disease that was controlling her.

Gram had Alzheimer's. The disease is cruel and relentless. While Alzheimer's does not affect a patient's health, it corrupts something even more precious: the mind. Alzheimer's stole Gram's thoughts and memories without her consent. Even worse, the disease grew more invasive with time, at first prompting almost imperceptible differences in Gram's behavior but eventually causing full-blown tantrums and extreme loss of memory. There was no cure. There still is no cure. There was not even a drug that could quell the effects of the disease, that could lessen Gram's suffering, or even that could mercifully speed the process. We were forced to watch Alzheimer's slowly consume Gram, taking its time. That was the hardest part of Gram's disease: watching Gram struggle against something more powerful than her. There was nothing we could do but wait.

Of all of us—my grandfather, my mom, my sister, Gram, and I—Gram was without a doubt the strongest. Her resilience never stopped amazing us. Each time we visited her, she would greet us with a sincere and radiant smile that did not betray a single note of pain. She would wrap me up in her warm embrace and whisper into my ear with a voice full of music and light, "You're a pearl of a girl." Gram lived in the moment, never allowing Alzheimer's to wholly defeat her. She maintained her wit, her passion and her love of life until her final moments. There was nothing Gram detested more than when others pitied her, and she made certain we rarely did. Gram epitomized perseverance. Never once did she stop fighting.

Sitting on my bedroom floor, still pressing Gram's robe into my face, I suddenly realized that the smooth silk no longer held Gram's grand scent. Instead, all I could smell was the odor of wood from my drawer. I realized I didn't even remember what Gram had smelled like anymore. The cruel irony of the thought struck me suddenly. Perhaps this was how Gram had felt, always struggling to grasp onto memories that just weren't there anymore. I sank back onto my hands and puzzled over the fragility of the human mind, the powerlessness of humans to combat the inevitable. I concluded that true strength arises when people accept that they are vulnerable but continue to ceaselessly overcome adversity. I could only hope to someday find this true strength within myself as entirely and fearlessly as Gram had.

•

"The girls," as Jane and I referred to Casey and Tara, were the grandchildren we naturally spent the most time with because Laura was *our child* and the one with whom we were the closest. I am sad and tearful as I read Casey's essay, so revealing of Jane and so clearly bringing back the joys and struggles of those years.

We spent Christmas with them each year until the last one or two and then they came to visit here after having Christmas at home. As Casey mentioned, Jane was intense about the gift paper, which toward the end became the focus of the occasion. I remember so clearly one of the last Christmases when Jane told me everything was black during the entire gift time. She had no memory of the event; she knew where the paper was.

•

Tara was thirteen when Jane died. She and Jane had a special relationship because Tara seemed dedicated to the world of art, a world which had captured Jane in high school, and then at the Moore Institute of Art. I include (with her permission and her mother's) something Tara wrote in the months following Jane's death.

A Hole in My Heart
Without Her
By Tara McConville

Every little thing reminds me of her.
A tree. A leaf. A song.
Almost like a candle.
Sometimes it is burning but other times the wick is cold and stiff.
Sometimes it burns brightly and other times the flame is dull and seconds away from burning out.
But then my life goes on and I forget about her.
The candle has flickered out and no longer provides light.
How? How do I live without her?
But there are always those times when she'll be all I can think about.
It's like a dream that keeps coming back.
But I don't cry. Why?
My eyes are sad and lonely but not wet.
Yet sometimes, only every so often, the world stops and it's like she's still here.
The flame on the now melting candle flickers back.
It waves around and blazes tall, sparking my memory.
I sit, blind to the world around me and cry.

Why her?
The world is so unfair.
Thoughts of what could have been flood my mind.
The flame burns out.
Only to restart the everlasting cycle.
This is my life without her.

Tara's deep emotional bond with Jane is apparent and I immediately associate it with my own. But for me, the candle flame never dims. It is the light that burns though the lonely times, the pleasant days, the whimsicality of life's encounters, and the memories of unleashed love and endless joy.

•

Although I've included some poems I've written, I never considered myself much of a poet. As many people my age do, I was going through some files and old papers recently. I discovered the original of a poem I wrote in 1957. I was an intern at Providence Hospital in Washington, D.C.

That year was the beginning of my unrest, my discomfort, but not yet my questioning in my marriage. Undoubtedly, it was also an opportunity, perhaps an incentive, to discover a more expansive world than I had known during the crammed and cramped world at Georgetown. Those four years were tightly lived. Classes were a constant challenge and life demanded supplementing our income with whatever jobs I could find.

Internship offered a less limited status and also allowed for a greater degree of interaction with patients, their family members, other interns, medical residents, and student nurses. During the internship year, I developed a close friendship with a student nurse and with a graduate nurse. These relationships seemed to contribute new meaning to my life. In retrospect, I have little doubt these interactions awakened some questions about my marriage and its future path.

This has been a roundabout way of getting to the poem I wrote during that internship year, 1957-58.

AN INTERN'S MEDITATION
Christ walked the halls last night
    And in His silent tread, a man lay dead.
He passed the corridor today

And in an infant's cry, life came by.

A mother prayed and wept beside her suffering son,
   But Christ was not asleep, He too can weep.
Another rested quietly with intravenous food,
   "I am the Bread, in Me there is no dead."

A scalpel cut through human flesh to prove
   Suffering is not chance, or why a soldier's lance?
A medicated needle caused one to cry in pain,
   Thorns caused blood to flow, can one say "No?"

A pre-op case abandoned hope and filled with fear.
   Christ will understand, and take his hand.
Another in lonely agony cried out, "Jesus Christ."
   But Jesus Christ is God, and God is good.

It surprised me to find this poem. It doesn't sound like who I was at that time. As I read it now, I wonder if I was praying for myself, if there were unacknowledged feelings, unformed thoughts that haunted me and brought the dreams I mentioned a few pages back (the ring of fire and the unknown woman in the car). Although I was invested in my patients even as an intern, these deeply spiritual reflections must have been based on something more personal.

   Individuals sometimes hide their emotional turmoil behind their spirituality. Anyone is quite capable of doing so. I used to find that subterfuge was not unusual among priests and nuns as well as other apparently devout persons. They are more likely to seek a spiritual director than a counselor. So, their "spiritual struggles" continue because they do not uncover and resolve the deeply seated but superficially denied emotional scars of their earlier life.

   Yes, I sought out a spiritual director as I mentioned. I did so primarily to resolve an emotional matter wrapped in a spiritual issue. When the spiritual concern was alleviated, the emotional impasse no longer continued to be an unresolved matter.

•

I have some personal theological thoughts I wish to share with you. When I was in grade school we had, of course, the *Baltimore Catechism.*

Question 1: Who made you?

God made me.

Question 2: How did God make you?

God made me in His own image and likeness.

The God we came to know through subsequent years was a Trinity, a Triune God, One God, but Three Persons. We know the *Trinity* cannot be fully explained. As I learned from the nuns, things that cannot be explained are called mysteries.

I'm not trying to sound erudite, but I'm comfortable with my understanding of the Trinity. I have used the expression more than once in this book: mind, body and spirit. I often pray for continued health of mind, body and spirit. That is my understanding of the Trinity. God the Father is the Creator, the Planner, as my mind is for me. God the Son is the Doer, the Worker, as my body is for me. God the Holy Spirit is the Inspirer, the Animator, as my spirit is for me.

•

Let me share another poem with you, a poem I recently wrote. Obviously, I continue to mourn the loss of Jane. I miss her and I'm lonely for her, but at the same time I'm pleased she rests in peace. The poem comes from my feelings when I take my walks.

CRY OF THE WIND
You seek your true love as you wander the earth,
You've loved her for long and treasured her worth
You comb through the grasses and fields of grain
You search and you search but you search in vain

Your quest goes on freely and wherever you will
If she's never found, you will search for her still
You imagine you see her but it's just a mirage
Your anger breeds violence and brings a barrage

Dark clouds of pain burst forth with your tears

The torrents of rain tell the depth of your fears
Your thunderous raging roars through the sky
The flashes of lighting scream Oh why, Oh why?

You dig deep in the ocean, throw water mid-air
You scatter the clouds and search if she's there
Sands of the desert are thrown hither and yon
Your cries speak lament She is gone, She is gone

Morning grasses are wet with dew from your eyes
And the fog of the evening helps muffle your sighs
Thru valleys and mountains on and on you must go
Your cries will continue, for *she is gone*, you know.

•

One day, probably a couple of years before Jane died, she came to my desk and gave me a small page from her tablet. It contained the following:

TO HIM I LOVE
Do you not see
That you and I
Are as the branches
Of one tree
With your rejoicing
Comes my laughter
With your sadness
Start my tears
Love, could life be otherwise
With you and me.

I read it and told her how beautiful I thought it was. I asked if she wrote it. She just quietly walked away and left me with it. I believe I've known it by heart since that day. It was so like her, so like us. It captured our life, our love. Ten lines describe the world we shared each day, each moment.

•

I walked today, the first day of autumn. A light jacket was comfortable. It was cool, cloudy and pleasant. I did some running, the first since the heat of summer. The rhythm and the energy required were invigorating and I found myself looking forward to cooler days and more of the same. It was another of those "thank you, God, for now and this."

•

Near the beginning of this book, I said there would be a quiz at the end. You have undoubtedly forgotten. You thought I would forget. But my endless proof reading repeatedly reminded me. So, here come the questions about those I introduced to you. Among the patients who impressed you most? Among those who were major figures in my life who did you wish you could have known? I said there would be multiple answers so you can pick as many as you like. I would say, "Anyone or all are good answers." If you're curious, in my mind Mary, the Native American, was the most significant patient; Father John Harvey, confessor and spiritual director, was the most significant person.

My mind tells me this book is coming to an end, but my heart protests "How can that be? We just started." Nearly a year has gone by since I wrote the first words. Does my heart object because I enjoy writing or because I enjoy writing about myself? I did enjoy writing about some of the patients I had, persons I appreciated, cared for, and about whom I have fond memories. I did enjoy writing about some of those fellow travelers to whom I am greatly indebted for their support, their encouragement, their wisdom and respect. I enjoyed writing about my parents, my friends, all those with whom I have indissoluble bonds of affection. Most of all, I enjoyed writing about Jane to whom I am boundlessly indebted for her life-changing love which graced my mind, my heart, my soul and continues to abide in my every moment of life.

Do I also enjoy writing about myself? I can't easily say yes. However, I do like to have people know more about me, not particularly the problems or negatives of my life, but the positive features I look back on and treasure. In writing, I often wondered if it sounded boastful. Perhaps it was. I take a certain pride in what I have accomplished, but I attribute any good I've done to the gifts of mind, body and spirit given and maintained by God's goodness. God gave me the tool box. I pray I used the tools well.

•

On my desk I have a much worn *The Spiral Memo Book*. It is 4 ¾ inches long and 2 ¾ inches wide. I used it during my college years, 1937—1941. I copied little things that appealed to me at the time. Why I entered two particular items raises an interesting question for me now. One item is Frederick Ozanam's *Prayer for a Perfect Wife*. The other was apparently untitled but was written by Mary Lavelle Kelley. The question I ask myself now is this: "Why did I copy these two pieces which are all about conjugal love?" I was a seminarian and had at least confirmed with my Bishop the priesthood as my choice.

As I now contemplate these various pieces of my life, finally put together as one whole, I find what seemed like insignificant events interwoven into an outcome I never could have anticipated, much less dreamed. I knew and liked a couple of girls during my college years *sub rosa*, as we would have said at the time. But my mindset and my spiritual goal was the priesthood. Apparently, my heart was not in total agreement. I'm sure I read these two items often during college years. I knew Ozanam's prayer by heart. I didn't realize: I wasn't reading them, *I was praying them*.

This is the apparently untitled verse.

> "It may be years before I see your face,
> And feel once more the warm sweet comfort
> Of your smile:
> It may be years before I touch your hand,
> And thrill unto the tenderness
> Of your embrace.
> It may be years. . .
> But what are years?
> And what are weary miles of space?
> When all the while, when all the while, my dear
> You dwell within my heart"
> A heart is such a safe, sure biding place."
> (Mary Lavelle Kelley)

Prayer for a Perfect Wife
"I feel within me an empty void, which neither friendship nor study can fill entirely. I know not who will fill this empty space, whether it be God or one of His creatures. If it be a

creature, I trust that she will not come too soon, before I have been able to render myself worthy of her. I trust that she will be endowed with all those necessary external graces so as not to leave room later for disillusionment. But above all I trust that she will possess solid virtues and a good heart, that she may be worth much more than I am and so draw me upwards rather than drag me downhill, that she may be resolute since I am faint-hearted, that she may be fervent since I am lukewarm, that she may be filled with a sense of compassion so that I may not feel too strongly in her presence my own sense of inferiority. These are my desires, these are my hopes."
(Frederick Ozanam)

I include these two pieces because they make a peaceful ending for my book. The first reveals my current state of mind. The second reveals the role my beloved Jane had in bringing me to the peace I have today. She *was* a perfect wife.

•

One last poem. I had forgotten I am a member of the national scholastic honor society, *Delta Epsilon Sigma*, as a result of graduating from Loras College *magna cum laude*. This poem of Matthew Browning appeared in the December 1979 issue of the *Delta Epsilon Sigma Journal*. I often thought of this second stanza as my epitaph.

> **AFTER AGAMEMNON**
> Mankind is more heroic than we know,
> And cries within:
> >"Measure me, yes, but measure me at my best.
> >Not by my denials, nor by my sins,
> >Nor by my death
> >(for these came easy)
> >But in one affirmation,
> >In one sacrifice of self to duty,
> >In one tick of timeless beauty,
> >See that I was in love.

>   The earth below, the sky above,
>   And all between were golden.
>   Once I walked ten feet tall, once I was wholly a man."
>   (Matthew Browning)

I close with the words of Francis of Assisi: "I am who I am in the eyes of God, nothing more, nothing less."

Acknowledgments

My gratitude to: Rev. Joe Heim, Dennis Mauro-Huse, and Sara Rubloff LCSW-C for their diligent reading of the manuscript, for valuable insights and their years of loving support.

Note for the Reader

Names and identifying characteristics mentioned in this book have been modified to protect the privacy of certain individuals.